Cambridge Elements

Elements in Generative AI in Education
edited by
Mark Warschauer
University of California, Irvine
Tamara Tate
University of California, Irvine

GENERATIVE AI IN COMPUTER SCIENCE EDUCATION

Challenges and Opportunities

Diana Franklin
University of Chicago

Paul Denny
The University of Auckland

David A. Gonzalez-Maldonado
The University of Chicago

Minh Tran
The University of Chicago

Shaftesbury Road, Cambridge CB2 8EA, United Kingdom

One Liberty Plaza, 20th Floor, New York, NY 10006, USA

477 Williamstown Road, Port Melbourne, VIC 3207, Australia

314–321, 3rd Floor, Plot 3, Splendor Forum, Jasola District Centre,
New Delhi – 110025, India

103 Penang Road, #05–06/07, Visioncrest Commercial, Singapore 238467

Cambridge University Press is part of Cambridge University Press & Assessment,
a department of the University of Cambridge.

We share the University's mission to contribute to society through the pursuit of
education, learning and research at the highest international levels of excellence.

www.cambridge.org
Information on this title: www.cambridge.org/9781009581691

DOI: 10.1017/9781009581738

When citing this work, please include a reference to the DOI 10.1017/9781009581738

First published 2025

A catalogue record for this publication is available from the British Library

ISBN 978-1-009-58169-1 Hardback
ISBN 978-1-009-58170-7 Paperback
ISSN 2977-3741 (online)
ISSN 2977-3733 (print)

Generative AI in Computer Science Education

Challenges and Opportunities

Elements in Generative AI in Education

DOI: 10.1017/9781009581738
First published online: April 2025

Diana Franklin
University of Chicago

Paul Denny
The University of Auckland

David A. Gonzalez-Maldonado
The University of Chicago

Minh Tran
The University of Chicago

Author for correspondence: Diana Franklin, dmfranklin@uchicago.edu

Abstract: Generative AI is a disruptive technology that has the potential to transform many aspects of how computer science is taught. Like previous innovations such as high-level programming languages and block-based programming languages, generative AI lowers the technical expertise necessary to create working programs, bringing the power of computation to more people. The programming process is already changing as a result of its presence, even for expert programmers. It also poses significant challenges to educators around rethinking assessment as some well-established approaches may no longer be viable. Many traditional programming assignments can be completed using generative AI tools with minimal effort, thus potentially undermining learning. In this Element, the authors explore both the opportunities and the challenges for computer science education resulting from the widespread availability of generative AI.

Keywords: computer science education, computing education, generative AI (GenAI), large language models (LLMs)

ISBNs: 9781009581691 (HB), 9781009581707 (PB), 9781009581738 (OC)
ISSNs: 2977-3741 (online), 2977-3733 (print)

Contents

1 Introduction

1.1 The Rise of Generative AI

Computer science education is undergoing a transformation as generative AI reshapes how we learn, teach, and create knowledge. Generative AI quickly advanced from niche to commodity in November 2022 with the launch of Chat-GPT by OpenAI (Thorbecke 2023). At the one-year anniversary of the launch, news outlets categorized ChatGPT as "Changing the Tech World" (Edwards 2023b) and starting an "AI Revolution" (Thorbecke 2023). In that first year, competitors also released AI chatbots, including Google's Bard and Amazon's Q (DeVon 2023). OpenAI also released DALL-E, software that produces artwork based on user-provided text prompts, in October 2023. More recently, the availability of multimodal models, which process and integrate multiple types of input such as text, images, and audio, has expanded rapidly, with both closed models (developed and maintained by private organizations and accessible only through web requests) and open models (freely accessible for use and for running on local hardware) contributing to the fast growing landscape of generative AI tools. The wide availability of such a range of generative AI models offers enormous potential for innovation, especially within education, but it also raises a number of pressing ethical questions.

One major concern is the use of copyrighted work to train models. Authors and artists have sued after their creative works have been used to train models that then produce similar outputs without compensation or credit (Edwards 2023a; Katersky 2023). Ethical concerns about generative AI have resulted in the United States' National Science Foundation issuing two major guidelines involving proposal creation and review (*Notice to research community: Use of generative artificial intelligence technology in the NSF merit review process* 2023). First, proposers are now "encouraged" to disclose the extent to which they used generative AI to develop their proposal. Second, reviewers are *prohibited* from uploading any content from proposals because of concerns that models may use that as training text. This could result in the model returning that same text to other users as responses to related prompts, breaching the confidentiality of the proposals and potentially leading to unintentional plagiarism.

Another major concern is how the use of generative AI may impact professionals, particularly regarding authorship and credit in academic and creative fields. For instance, the Writers Guild of America held a 148-day strike partly over disagreements related to credit and income due to the increasing use of generative AI in scriptwriting (Coyle 2023). In addition, some companies have replaced customer service representatives with ChatGPT because it responded to customer questions as well or better than many customer service agents (Verma 2023). In the academic sphere, policies are evolving to address these concerns; for example, the Association of Computing Machinery (ACM) stipulates that while generative AI tools like ChatGPT can be used to create content, their use must be fully disclosed in an acknowledgments section, and they cannot be listed as authors of a published work.

Finally, there are examples from several fields of authors using ChatGPT and passing off its output as their own writing, then being subsequently discovered due to inaccuracies in the information that ChatGPT returns. For example, two lawyers and their firm were fined for submitting formal court documents generated by ChatGPT that contained fictitious legal research (Neumeister 2023). Vanderbilt University faced backlash after it sent an email to students reflecting on a tragic shooting at Michigan State University, which was later revealed to have been drafted using ChatGPT – a decision widely criticized for its perceived lack of genuine human empathy (Powers 2023). Similarly, recent controversies have arisen with the use of other generative AI tools in creative and commercial contexts, such as advertisements for Google Gemini (that suggested using it to draft personal letters) and for Toys 'R' Us (which used OpenAI's Sora model to generate a full-length video), both of which sparked debates about the erosion of human creativity and authenticity. A judge in Colombia even asked ChatGPT for help with case law, asking, "Is an autistic minor exonerated from paying fees for their therapies?" to which ChatGPT responded, "Yes, this is correct. According to the regulations in Colombia, minors diagnosed with autism are exempt from paying fees for their therapies" (Stanly 2023). Although this response agreed with the judge's decision, the use of ChatGPT for guiding legal decisions generated criticism at the time.

1.2 Challenges and Opportunities in Education

In the field of education in general, there are major concerns about students using ChatGPT to cheat. A BestCollegesSurvey of 10,000 current undergraduate and graduate students found that 51 percent of college students believe that using such tools for assignments and exams is cheating, compared with only 20 percent who disagreed (Nietzel 2023). In early 2023, coinciding with the first school term where ChatGPT was widely available and well known, concerns were voiced on a national scale. Many instructors at Harvard prohibited students from using ChatGPT, considering it a form of academic dishonesty (Duffy and Weil 2023), and articles hypothesized about using it for cheating (Vicci 2023). There may be some data to back up this hypothesis – use of ChatGPT tailed off in June 2023, corresponding with summer break, then increased again in September (Barr 2023). Some good news, however, is that an annual survey performed by Stanford researchers showed that the percentage of high school students reporting that they engaged in at least one "cheating" behavior in the past month had remained unchanged (Spector 2023). This suggests that while the tools may change, new technologies may not necessarily be encouraging a greater proportion of students to use them dishonestly.

The field of computer science has not been immune to legal controversies regarding AI-based code generation. For instance, a class action lawsuit was filed in November 2022 against GitHub Copilot by a group of software engineers, alleging that GitHub, Microsoft, and OpenAI violated copyright, privacy, and business laws by using copyrighted developer source code without permission to train their models (Park et al. 2023). The plaintiffs argued that Copilot often produced code suggestions that were identical to the original copyrighted works without proper attribution or consent. Although GitHub and its partners contested these claims, the lawsuit raised ethical and legal questions about AI's reliance on publicly available code. Despite such controversies, discussions in the popular media around tools like GitHub Copilot and ChatGPT often focus on their performance and providing guidance on their use, rather than focusing on the ethical implications of AI-generated code or predicting significant job losses within the computing industry.

From an academic perspective, large language models (LLMs) were first considered by the computer science education community in February 2022, at the Australasian Computing Education conference, when Finnie-Ansley et al. presented their paper "The Robots are Coming: Exploring the Implications of OpenAI Codex on Introductory Programming" (Finnie-Ansley et al. 2022). This was the first paper published in a computing education venue that explicitly assessed the capabilities of an LLM designed for code generation, OpenAI's Codex, when applied to standard introductory programming (CS1) problems. The paper compared the performance of the Codex model to the performance of a cohort of students on the same set of programming problems, finding that the model's performance would see it rank in the 17th position out of a class of 71 students. In addition, an analysis involving several variations of the classic "Rainfall" problem (Fisler 2014) revealed that from the same input prompt, the Codex model would produce multiple unique solutions varied in length, syntax, and algorithmic approach. The authors concluded this work by stating

> "we have examined what could be considered an emergent existential threat to the teaching and learning of introductory programming. With some hesitation we have decided to state how we truly feel – the results are stunning – demonstrating capability far beyond that expected by the authors." (p. 18).

This paper appeared at a time when awareness of generative AI was not yet widespread in the academic community, and thus set the stage for a broader discussion of the implications of this new technology for educators and for classroom practice.

Subsequent discussion and position papers, including those by Denny, Prather, et al. (2024), Becker et al. (2023), and Prather, Denny et al. (2023), have further explored both the opportunities and challenges that LLMs present to computing education. Among the challenges highlighted are concerns related to academic integrity, such as the potential for increased plagiarism and unauthorized code use; the danger of students becoming too reliant on AI, which might hinder their understanding of core programming concepts; and the risk of novices being misled by inappropriate or confusing outputs. In contrast, the opportunities presented by LLMs may be transformative. The ability to generate high-quality educational resources, provide instant feedback, and shift the educational focus toward solving more complex, engaging problems rather than a more narrow focus on low-level coding and related syntax issues represents potentially significant positive changes for computing education.

1.3 Stucture and Audience

In this Element, we consider and discuss the ways in which generative AI (GenAI) could be used in computer science education, both positive and negative. While computer science instruction covers a broad set of topics, including but not limited to how hardware and networks work, how to code, how to analyze code, and how to prove properties of code, most of the existing efforts and literature have focused on tertiary-level coding courses. As a result, much of the related work that is discussed in our Element focuses on the use of LLMs in such contexts. We do, however, provide some insights into the challenges and opportunities for using LLMs more broadly, such as in K–12 education or for instruction on specific topics such as formal proofs.

This Element is written with several audiences in mind. Educators not familiar with large language models can gain insight into the impacts, both positive and negative, of their uses, as well as some of the strategies people are exploring that range from embracing their use to mitigating the downsides of their use. For this audience, we have included some background on how large language models work, and we define vocabulary as it arises. Computer science education researchers who are interested in entering this emerging research area will learn about the latest research and where to seek additional information.

For this audience, we have carefully cited the research we describe, including much of the most recent work published as of August 2024.

We begin in Section 2 by providing insight into how large language models work, starting with more simple technologies that are easier to reason about and ending with their current capabilities with respect to computer science education. We then describe the key findings of several studies on both instructor and student perceptions of the use of generative AI in computer science classrooms in Section 3.

The next part of the Element explores current uses of generative AI. First, we present a variety of ways instructors could use generative AI tools to improve the way that they *prepare for instruction* (Section 4). Then, in Section 5, we explore a range of uses of generative AI tools *during instruction*. Finally, we discuss how to integrate these separate capabilities into unified *end-user tools* in Section 6.

The final part of this Element tackles bigger implications of the technology. Section 7 discusses how learners and educators may be impacted by students' misuse of generative AI tools. Then, in Section 8, we look to the future and consider how computer science education might change in response to the adoption of GenAI in industry. If industry is embracing generative AI coding tools, what different skills should we be teaching to help computer science students be the most efficient, skilled software developers upon graduation? Finally, we present a case study of a course designed and piloted at the University of California, San Diego, which fully embraces the use of generative AI. This innovative course defines learning goals that match industry needs in the presence of generative AI tools and includes training for students on GitHub Copilot, as well as the integration of more ambitious and interesting coding projects made possible due to the availability of Copilot. The course also adjusts how assessments are run and graded to provide a balance between encouraging the use of Copilot and ensuring that students are still learning the necessary technical material.

2 Understanding Large Language Models and ChatGPT

To better understand the strengths and weaknesses of chatbots such as Chat-GPT, we begin by providing a brief introduction to the technology. We start by presenting a related technology – a machine learning image classifier. We then discuss LLMs, along with some of their common behaviors. Finally, we provide a summary of evaluations of the capabilities of LLMs for performing coding-related tasks.

Vocabulary

Image Classifier: A machine learning model designed to classify or recognize objects, animals, or other entities in images by analyzing their visual features, such as a giraffe, bus, or person's face.

Generative AI: Artificial intelligence models that generate new content, such as text, images, audio, or video, based on learned patterns from large datasets.

Large Language Models (LLMs): A type of generative AI model trained on large text datasets to produce coherent and contextually appropriate text outputs by generating sequences of "tokens" (words or phrases).

ChatGPT: A conversational large language model (LLM) developed by OpenAI and designed to generate human-like responses in a dialogue format.

Hallucination: A phenomenon where a large language model generates incorrect or nonsensical responses that appear plausible but are not grounded in its training data or factual information.

2.1 Image Classifier

An image classifier is a program that can recognize images, such as a giraffe, bus, or person's face. Creating an image classifier consists of two phases: training and use.

The training phase is how the classifier learns to associate attributes of the image with the results. In order to train a classifier, a database of pictures that have already been "labeled" (tagged with what is in the picture) is needed. For example, if an "animal" classifier is wanted, then a database of pictures with different types of animals is required, each labeled with the type of animal in the picture. For a vehicle classifier, a database of pictures with different types of vehicles is needed, each labeled with the type of vehicle in the picture. A program analyzes the database of pictures, determining the characteristics that distinguish, say, pictures of motorcycles from pictures of trucks.

The attributes of the training set are a critical component of the accuracy of the trained model. A "good" training set would include a wide variety of instances for each type of item – including different colors, camera angles, and other features. Not surprisingly, the more labeled images an image classifier has, the more accurate it is at classifying images. In addition, an image classifier is unable to place something in a category for which it was not trained without extra computation. If the training set is too small, then the classifier might get trained on "red herrings" – attributes that just happen to be in the pictures. For example, if someone trained the animal classifier on snakes that all live in the desert and squirrels that all live in the forest, then a picture of a snake in a forest might be identified as a squirrel, and a picture of a squirrel in a desert might be identified as a snake.

Some databases may even contain pictures that have been labeled unknowingly. For example, to automatically tag a particular friend when a picture is uploaded to Facebook®, Facebook needs an image classifier. Its training data on a specific friend would consist of all the pictures of that friend that have been labeled by users. Additionally, completing security puzzles by Captcha, such as clicking on all the boxes in a picture that contain traffic lights, motorcycles, or trucks, contributes labeled images to improve an image classifier.

There are major ethical concerns with image recognition being used for facial recognition of humans because of the interaction between people of color, the inaccuracy of models on those people, and historical injustices. Clearview AI has gone a step further than Facebook, mining social media to create an extensive database of images and names, leading to a proposed fine by the Netherlands (Corder 2024). The database is marketed to law enforcement to identify suspects in crimes, which raises ethical questions, since the data is not verified to be correct, and arrests of innocent civilians have occurred because of misidentification in such systems (Johnson 2023). Facial recognition has been shown to be especially poor on individuals with darker skin (Sanford 2024); this could be because of either poor training sets or the challenge of distinguishing their features in poor lighting. Therefore, one must consider not only the technological perspective of AI, but also its impact on different populations.

2.2 Large Language Models

Large language models are a type of artificial intelligence model designed to generate text by predicting the next word, or "token," in a sequence. Unlike image classifiers, which rely on labeled datasets to learn from, LLMs use a method called *self-supervised learning*. In self-supervised learning, the model learns from vast amounts of text data without needing explicit labels. Instead, the model uses parts of the text to predict other parts (enabling it to verify these predictions automatically), making the process of data preparation more scalable and efficient.

So, in essence, an LLM simply predicts tokens (or words). Consider a very basic sentence (which we can think of as a "prompt"), which is incomplete:

Prompt: "The cat sat on the"

An LLM is able to predict the most likely next word (token) to follow the sequence "The cat sat on the". It does this by considering the context and calculating the probability distribution for all possible next words it has learned from its training. Based on the patterns it has learned, the model might generate a frequency distribution like "mat": 60 percent, "floor": 20 percent, "chair": 10 percent, "table": 5 percent, "roof": 3 percent, and so on.

In this example, the word "mat" has the highest probability (60 percent) because the phrase "The cat sat on the mat" is a common phrase the model has likely seen many times in its training data. Therefore, the model is most likely to select "mat" as the next word. However, one parameter of an LLM is the "temperature" value, and this setting controls the randomness of the output. Thus, it might occasionally choose another word like "floor" or "chair," and would be more likely to do so with a higher "temperature" setting. Finally, after selecting "mat," the LLM can repeat the process all over again – thus generating a coherent sentence that aligns with the patterns it has learned from its training data.

During training, an LLM analyzes large datasets comprising diverse types of text, such as books, articles, and web content. Because LLMs are trained to predict tokens based on their context, they can generate a wide range of text outputs, from simple factual answers to more complex tasks like writing essays, generating code, or summarizing long documents. However, they are not perfect; their outputs are based on probabilities derived from their training data, which means they can sometimes generate inaccurate or even nonsensical responses, often referred to as "hallucinations."

One of the most well-known tools that uses an LLM to generate text is ChatGPT, developed by OpenAI. ChatGPT leverages the LLM architecture and generates human-like responses by predicting tokens that fit well in a conversation. To make its responses more useful, safe, and aligned with what a human would expect, OpenAI used a technique called Reinforcement Learning from Human Feedback (RLHF). In this process, human trainers rated the model's responses, giving positive feedback for answers that align well with conversational norms and factual accuracy, and negative feedback for responses that were misleading or unhelpful.

The probabilistic generation of tokens helps explain some of the strengths and weaknesses of ChatGPT. If there are many examples in the training set similar to what is being generated, the model can draw from a robust probability distribution, resulting in highly accurate and predictable outputs. For example, the question "is the world round?" will likely result in the output "Yes," as this is a common question–answer pair in the training data. Similarly, asking ChatGPT to finish a series of fairly unique, famous quotes that would have appeared

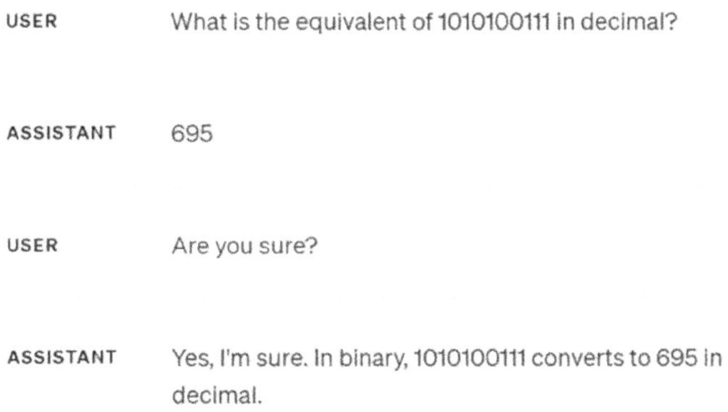

USER   What is the equivalent of 1010100111 in decimal?

ASSISTANT   695

USER   Are you sure?

ASSISTANT   Yes, I'm sure. In binary, 1010100111 converts to 695 in
                decimal.

Figure 1 A modern LLM appearing "confidently incorrect" (screenshot from March 2024). The correct answer is 679.

many times in its training set typically results in the expected output. For example: "With great power" …"comes great responsibility" (Spider-Man); "Don't let the muggles" …"get you down" (Harry Potter). For more complex tasks that do not have direct matches in the training data, ChatGPT relies on its ability to detect and combine patterns it has learned during training. For instance, if asked to generate a resume for a specific computer scientist, ChatGPT might draw on general information about typical resume structures and content it has seen, as well as any relevant information it has learned about computer scientists in general. The result is a resume that appears plausible and well-structured. However, because ChatGPT generates content based on patterns rather than specific knowledge, the output may contain a mix of both accurate and inaccurate information. This blending of learned patterns allows ChatGPT to produce creative and contextually appropriate text, but it also means that users need to verify the details to ensure they are correct.

As mentioned earlier, when an LLM provides an incorrect answer to a factual question, it is sometimes called a *hallucination*. Another interesting characteristic of LLMs is that they are sometimes characterized as producing responses that are *confidently incorrect*. This refers to ChatGPT answering a question incorrectly with the same wording and confidence as answering a question accurately, with no mitigating language that a human might use (e.g., "I'm not sure, but this might be the answer"). See, for example, the output in Figure 1. Viewing LLMs as probabilistically generating answers that fit the pattern again explains this trend. ChatGPT was built to generate *likely* answers that fit a pattern, not *factual* answers. Therefore, it is always necessary to fact-check what an LLM produces, even when it does not "admit" to being unsure. This can have negative effects if people are not aware of these limitations. For example, Chat-GPT has been shown to produce inaccurate responses when asked questions about drug information; ChatGPT's answers to nearly three-quarters of drug-related questions reviewed by pharmacists were incomplete or wrong. In one case, researchers asked ChatGPT whether a drug interaction exists between the COVID-19 antiviral Paxlovid and the blood-pressure-lowering medication verapamil, and ChatGPT indicated no interactions had been reported for this combination of drugs (ASHP 2023).

While LLMs like ChatGPT are updated periodically, they do not continuously scrape the internet for new information. Instead, they are retrained on new datasets at regular intervals, incorporating updated knowledge and fine-tuning from user interactions and feedback. However, promising techniques are emerging for improving the accuracy of LLM-generated responses in specific contexts. One effective approach is Retrieval-Augmented Generation (RAG), which combines the power of LLMs with external databases. Unlike traditional LLMs, which rely solely on their training data, RAG allows the model to retrieve relevant information from an external database or knowledge source before generating a response. This means that instead of guessing based on patterns it has seen during training, the model can refer to up-to-date or domain-specific information to provide more accurate and contextually relevant answers. For example, a model enhanced with RAG could retrieve the latest medical guidelines to answer a question about drug interactions more reliably. Another advancement in LLM technology is the use of chain-of-thought prompting, a method inspired by how humans approach complex problems. Instead of generating a single, immediate answer, the model explicitly articulates its reasoning process step by step before arriving at its final output. Such an approach can improve the ability of the model for tackling difficult or multistep problems, and by showing these steps it makes its reasoning more apparent to users.

2.3 LLMs for Coding

What about generating source code for a program? Large language models have been trained on enormous quantities of publicly accessible code from GitHub repositories and programming tutorials on the web (M. Chen et al. 2021). Given that programming languages have a much smaller set of grammatical rules than, say, natural languages, LLMs are especially good at producing code that is syntactically correct. In addition, their ability to make predictions based on context (such as detailed problem specifications) means they are often highly capable of producing correct solutions to programming problems.

A focus of much of the early work within the computing education community involved exploring the breadth of problems to which generative AI models could be applied. However, measuring the capabilities of such models is challenging given the rapid pace at which improvements are being made. For example, the results from "The Robots Are Coming" paper published in February 2022 (Finnie-Ansley et al. 2022) were replicated in July 2023 – less than 18 months later – by a working group exploring LLMs in the context of computing education (Prather, Denny et al. 2023). Compared to the original performance of the Codex model (which scored an average of 78.3% across two exams), the GPT-4 model (which was the state-of-the-art model at the time of the working group's replication) exhibited dramatic improvement, scoring an average of 97% over two programming exams.

In general, LLMs have shown considerable proficiency in programming tasks, even beyond typical CS1-type problems. For example, Cipriano and Alves (2023) explored object-oriented programming (OOP) assignments, where students are typically asked to follow a set of best practices to design and implement a suite of interrelated classes (either by composition or inheritance). Using the GPT-3 model, they found that it was able to generate code that would achieve good scores when evaluated against unit tests, but that minor compilation and logic errors were still somewhat common. Interestingly, the specifications for the assignments that they evaluated were written in Portuguese, which did not appear to negatively impact performance despite the fact that Portuguese content makes up only a very small fraction of the model training sets.[1] Similarly, in follow-up work to their original paper, Finnie-Ansley et al. (2023) explored the performance of the Codex model on a collection of CS2 problems from a standard data structures and algorithms course. They found that when compared to the performance of students who had tackled the same problems on a test, the Codex model's performance would place it just within the top quartile of the class.

Of course, while code-writing questions are common, there are many other kinds of problems of relevance to computing courses. For example, multiple-choice questions are in common use in large classes and are frequently used to assess code comprehension skill (Petersen, Craig, and Zingaro 2011). Savelka et al.'s investigation into the evolving efficacy of LLMs from GPT-3 to GPT-4 highlights a progressive improvement in answering multiple-choice questions for programming classes (Savelka, Agarwal, An et al. 2023; Savelka et al. (2023). This suggests an increasing capacity of these models to mimic, if not surpass, human-level understanding in standard assessment formats.

Another question format that is unique to programming education is Parsons problems, which require the rearrangement of initially scrambled lines of code (Ericson et al. 2022). Unlike code-writing questions, where a code-generating

---

[1] https://commoncrawl.github.io/cc-crawl-statistics/plots/languages

AI model has the flexibility to synthesize code one token at a time based on the preceding tokens, Parsons problems provide the constraint that a solution must be formed using only the code blocks provided. Reeves et al. (2023) examined the performance of the Codex model on a suite of Parsons problems obtained from a review of the literature. They found that the model could successfully solve around half of the Parsons problems, and observed that Codex would very rarely modify or add new lines of code, but that incorrectly indenting the code was the most common reason for failure. This investigation into solving Parsons problems with text-based models was complemented by the work of Hou et al. (2024), exploring the capabilities of so-called 'vision' models that could be provided with a bitmap version of a Parsons problem produced via a screenshot. In a comparison of two popular multimodal models, they found that at the time of their evaluation, GPT-4V clearly outperformed Bard, solving around 97% of the problems presented to it. Hou et al. conclude that the use of visual-based problems by educators, as a way to reduce student reliance on text-based LLMs for solving coursework, is unlikely to be a viable solution in the long term. They also recommend that computing educators reconsider their assessment practices in light of such impressive model performance.

3 Educator and Student Perceptions

Given the rapidly evolving capabilities of generative AI tools, it is essential to understand how they are perceived by both educators and students within the context of computing education. Several studies have shed light on these perceptions, revealing a complex landscape of excitement, concern, and adaptation strategies.

3.1 Educator Perceptions

Educator views on generative AI tools span a spectrum that is nicely captured in the title of the paper by Lau and Guo: "From 'Ban It Till We Understand It' to 'Resistance is Futile.'" (Lau and Guo 2023). In this work, they investigated the perspectives of university programming instructors on adapting their courses in response to the increasing use among students of AI code generation and explanation tools like ChatGPT and GitHub Copilot. Conducted in early 2023, this research involved semistructured interviews with 20 introductory programming instructors from diverse geographic locations and institution types. By focusing on exploring immediate reactions and longer-term plans, the study aimed to gather a broad spectrum of strategies and viewpoints on integrating or resisting AI coding tools in educational settings. In the short term, instructors were predominantly concerned about AI-assisted cheating, leading to immediate measures like placing a greater emphasis on exam scores, banning AI tools, and exposing students to the tools' capabilities and limitations. Looking further ahead, instructors diverged into two main camps: those aiming to resist AI tool usage, focusing on teaching programming fundamentals, and those embracing AI tools, viewing them as preparation for future job environments. This division underscores the lack of consensus and the exploratory nature of current approaches to AI in computing education.

Strategies to resist AI tool usage included designing "AI-proof" assignments, reverting to paper-based exams, and emphasizing code reading and critique over programming tasks. Instructors who were more open to integrating AI tools proposed using these technologies to offer personalized learning experiences, assisting with teaching tasks, and redefining the curriculum with a greater emphasis on software design, collaboration with AI, and creative project work. Overall, the findings suggest a need for adaptive teaching strategies that either incorporate AI as a tool for learning and development or reinforce traditional coding skills in novel ways that are resistant to trivial LLM-generated solutions. Lau and Guo also proposed a diverse set of open research questions that help plot a course for continued investigation within the community.

In more recent work, Sheard et al. (2024) conducted interviews with 12 instructors from Australia, Finland, and New Zealand. These interviews aimed to capture a diverse set of perspectives on the use of AI tools in computing education, including current practices and planned modifications in response to AI tools. In general, instructors acknowledged the potential of AI tools to support and enhance learning by generating code examples and providing personalized feedback. However, concerns were raised about students potentially bypassing crucial learning processes and over-relying on these tools, which could lead to a shallow understanding of programming concepts. Participants also noted significant challenges to traditional assessment methods, raising concerns about academic integrity and the potential for cheating. Such concerns are exemplified in the following quote from one participant in the study: "we are clearly living in a time in which we have to completely rethink computing education, and particularly the assessment side of computing education, because we can no longer assess students in any of the ways we have been trying to assess them." There was general agreement from the participants of this interview study that the integration of AI tools should be at a point in the curriculum where students have already acquired foundational programming skills. Note, this view is not universal within the community, with some researchers suggesting a "prompts first" approach, in which students begin by learning to prompt AI models, is what is needed (Reeves et al. 2024).

3.2 Student Perceptions

Students appear to share some of the same concerns as educators. Prather, Reeves, et al. (2023) provide an insightful exploration into novice programmers' interactions with GitHub Copilot. Students reported a mix of awe and unease, with some finding the tool's predictiveness both helpful and unsettling. This latter feeling, which inspired the title of their paper, was typified in the comment from one student: "I thought it was weird that it knows what I want." While Copilot was praised for its ability to streamline coding tasks, concerns were raised regarding overreliance on the tool and potential barriers to learning fundamental problem-solving skills. One participant even expressed concern that the tool would make them a "worse problem solver" as they begin to rely on it more. Additionally, the study unveiled cognitive and metacognitive challenges students face, prompting a discussion on the need for educational tools to better support learning processes.

A comprehensive report of an ITiCSE Working Group that convened in July 2023 combined insights from a broad survey involving both educators and students across 17 countries (Prather, Denny et al. 2023). Two separate surveys were developed for students and instructors, covering topics from generative AI tool use and ethical considerations to perceived impacts on education and future employment. Both groups reported similar patterns in using generative AI for code writing and for text-based tasks, indicating a growing familiarity with these technologies. There was also a strong consensus on the irreplaceable role of human instructors despite acknowledging the growing relevance of generative AI tools in computing education and future careers. Especially among upper-level students, generative AI tools appear to be becoming a significant resource for student assistance, indicating a shift in help-seeking preferences. Among the implications of this work, as identified by the report authors, is that educators should be aware of technological advancements so that they can effectively integrate generative AI tools into their teaching practices.

4 Class Preparation

One way that computing educators can clearly leverage generative AI is in the creation of high-quality learning resources. Such resources can be static (i.e. generated in bulk and distributed via an appropriate platform) or dynamic (i.e. generated on demand by students). Among the many possible resources that can be produced by generative AI tools, code explanations, programming exercises, and worked examples have recently been proposed and studied. In this section, we first present traditional teaching techniques, followed by the ways in which LLMs can assist.

4.1 Example Code Explanations

We first consider textbook examples. MacNeil et al. (2023), integrated LLM-generated *code explanations* into an interactive e-book on web software development. Three types of explanations were generated for code snippets: line-by-line explanations, a list of important concepts, and a high-level summary. Table 1 shows examples of explanations generated by GPT-3 for a code snippet to create a simple server that counts the number of POST requests. The line-by-line explanation (a) highlights aspects of the syntax and terminology in every line of code, the listing concepts (b) are explanations of important concepts used in the code, whereas the summarization (c) provides a high-level explanation of the purpose of the code.

They found that student engagement varied based on code snippet complexity, explanation type, and snippet length, but that overall the majority of students found the code explanations helpful. Similarly, Leinonen, Denny, et al. (2023) compared the quality of code explanations generated by students and LLMs in a CS1 course context, finding that students rated LLM-created explanations as significantly easier to understand and more accurate summaries of code than those created by students. Both studies highlight the potential of LLMs as tools for generating educational content in computing courses. There remain, however, some concerns regarding the accuracy and completeness of LLM-generated code explanations, indicating the need for oversight or additional processing before these explanations are presented to learners.

4.2 Worked Examples

Worked examples have been well researched in introductory programming courses (Muldner, Jennings, and Chiarelli (2022)). Worked examples involve a problem statement with a step-by-step annotated solution that illustrates the problem-solving process (see Table 2). Worked examples can take several forms.

Modeled worked examples occur during a lecture. An instructor writes code, narrating their thought process as they do so. They may make mistakes, requiring them to make modifications in real-time. The alternative is to provide static code all at once, explaining how it works after it is all displayed. The effectiveness of such modeling is unclear. In one study, modeling examples led to no differences between groups on exams, assignments, and overall course scores; a benefit was only observed on the final course project (Rubin 2013). In another study, there were no significant differences (Raj et al. 2020). LLMs may not be obviously appropriate for this kind of modeling, given that they generate

Table 1 Examples of three types of code explanations generated by GPT-3 for a code snippet for a server that counts POST requests; adapted from MacNeil et al. (2023).

```
import { serve } from "https://deno.land/std@0.140.0/http/server.ts";
let count = 0;
const handleRequest = (request) => {
    if (request.method === "POST") {
        count++;
    }
    return new Response(count);
}
serve(handleRequest, { port: 7777 });
```

(a) Line-by-Line

- The first line imports the 'serve' function from the 'server' module in the 'std' library from version 0.140.0 of the Deno runtime.
- The second line declares a 'count' variable and initializes it to 0.
- The second line defines a 'handleRequest' function that takes a 'request' parameter. This function increments the value of 'count' if the 'request' method is 'POST'.
- The fourth line returns a new 'Response' object containing the value of 'count'.
- The fifth line calls the 'serve' function, passing in the 'handleRequest' function and an options object. The options object sets the 'port' property to 7777.

(b) Listing concepts

1. Modules: The code uses the "server" module from the standard library to create a server and handle requests.
2. Functions: The "handleRequest" function is used to handle incoming requests and return a response.
3. Conditional statements: The code checks if the request method is "POST" and increments the count if it is.
4. Variables: The "count" variable is used to keep track of the number of POST requests received.
5. Response: The "Response" object is used to send a response back to the client.
6. Ports: The server is configured to listen to port 7777.

(c) Summary

This code snippet creates a server that listens for POST requests on port 7777. For each POST request received, the server increments a counter and returns the current value of the counter in the response.

Table 2 An exemplar step-by-step worked example of the problem: *Write a Python program to print out the maximum value in a 2-d array*

Step 1: Initialize the variable to store the maximum value

max_value = array[0][0]

Step 2: Iterate through the array

```
max_value = array[0][0]
for row in array:
    for element in row:
```

Step 3: Compare each element and update the maximum value

```
max_value = array[0][0]
for row in array:
    for element in row:
        if element > max_value:
            max_value = element
```

Step 3: Print out the output

```
max_value = array[0][0]
for row in array:
    for element in row:
        if element > max_value:
            max_value = element
print(max_value)
```

static text. However, with an appropriate display interface it may be possible to use an LLM – perhaps including and correcting some deliberate mistakes – to simulate a teacher modeling a worked example. Indeed, Jury et al. (2024) evaluated a novel LLM-powered worked example tool in an introductory programming course. Their tool, "WorkedGen", leveraged an LLM to generate interactive *worked examples* in a large first-year Python programming course to evaluate the quality and effectiveness of the LLM-generated worked examples. The evaluation focused on the clarity of explanations, the breakdown of worked examples into well-defined steps, and the tool's overall usefulness to novice programmers. In general, the LLM-generated explanations were clear, and the code provided alongside explanations was deemed valuable. In the classroom deployment, students expressed that the LLM-generated worked examples were useful for their learning, indicating a positive perception of the tool. In particular, students appreciated the ability to engage further with a given worked example by selecting keywords, code lines, and personalized questions, which were custom features within the tool.

The bulk of research on worked examples in introductory coding instruction has been on supplementing example solutions with subgoals. Subgoals are high-level statements about the purpose of the example solution steps. Worked examples with subgoals have been found to be beneficial in several settings. An initial study compared examples annotated with subgoals (create component, set output, set conditions, define variables) to unannotated examples for students learning to create Android App Inventor programs. The researchers found significantly better results on both an immediate post-test and a delayed post-test (Margulieux, Catrambone, and Guzdial (2016)). A lab replication study involving university students replicated the results (Margulieux and Catrambone 2016). A more realistic classroom setting found that the sections with subgoal-annotated worked examples performed significantly better on quizzes and had a lower dropout rate (Margulieux, Morrison, and Decker (2020)).

4.3 Programming Exercises

One of the first papers in the computing education literature to explore the generation of learning resources focused on programming exercises. Traditionally, there have been four major categories of programming exercises that assess and develop student skills: Tracing, Explain in Plain English (EiPE), Parson's Problems, and coding problems (see Figures 2–5).

Sarsa et al. (2022) explored the creation of *programming exercises* with sample solutions and test cases, as well as code explanations. The rationale behind the research stems from the challenges educators face in developing a comprehensive set of novel exercises and the demand for active learning opportunities

Assuming input a = [3, 6, 8, 2, 4, 6, 9],
len = 7, what value is returned by func?

```
int func(int array[], int len) {
    int x = array[0];
    int i = 0;
    for ( i = 0; i < len; i++) {
        if (array[i] < x)
            x = array[i];
    }
    return x;
}
```

Figure 2 Tracing

Explain in your own words what the
following function does:

```c
int func(int array[], int len) {
    int x = array[0];
    int i = 0;
    for ( i = 0; i < len; i++) {
        if (array[i] < x)
            x = array[i];
    }
    return x;
}
```

Figure 3 Explain in Plain English (EiPE)

Reorder the following lines of code
to create a function that returns the
maximum value in an array. That is,
with inputs a = [3, 6, 8, 2, 4, 6, 9]
and len = 7, it would return 9.

```c
int func(int array[], int len) {
if (array[i] < x)
int x;
int i = 0;
for ( i = 0; i < len; i++) {
x = array[0];
}
return x;
x = array[i];
}
```

Figure 4 Parsons

Write a function max that takes an
integer array and its length and
returns the maximum value in the array.
With inputs a = [3, 6, 8, 2, 4, 6, 9]
and len = 7, it would return 9.

```c
int max(int array[], int len) {



}
```

Figure 5 Coding

in programming education. A total of 240 programming exercises were generated, and a subset was evaluated both qualitatively and quantitatively for the sensibleness, novelty, and readiness for use of the generated content. The authors found that a significant majority of the automatically generated programming exercises were both sensible and novel, with many being ready to use with minimal modifications. They also found that it was possible to influence the content of the exercises effectively by specifying both programming concepts and contextual themes in the input to the Codex model. The ability to contextualize learning resources could potentially lead to more personalized and engaging learning experiences, especially if exercises can be tailored to individual interests through contextual themes (Del Carpio Gutierrez, Denny, and Luxton-Reilly (2024); Leinonen, Denny, and Whalley (2021)). While most of the generated exercises included sample solutions and automated tests, the quality of the test cases was variable, and in some instances, the tests did not entirely align with the solutions, suggesting the need for some manual intervention or regeneration of tests. Future research directions posed by the authors include refining the generation process to improve test case quality, and exploring the generation of more complex exercises and assignments, as well as investigating student engagement and learning outcomes when using automatically generated content. Recent work exploring the generation of test cases has been promising; for example, Alkafaween et al. (2024) demonstrated that LLM-generated test suites for CS1-level programming problems are not only able to correctly identify most valid student solutions but are also, in many cases, as comprehensive as instructor-created test suites.

4.4 Block-Based Programming Assignments

Culturally Competent Projects

> VOCABULARY
>
> **Culturally Responsive Pedagogy**: A learner-centered approach to teaching that incorporates students' cultural identities and lived experiences into the classroom to facilitate their engagement and academic success.
>
> **Cultural Competence**: The ability of an individual to honor their cultural backgrounds while developing understanding in at least one other culture.
>
> **Reskinning**: The process of modifying the visual presentation of a Scratch project by changing the sprites and backdrop to match with a new theme while keeping the code untouched.

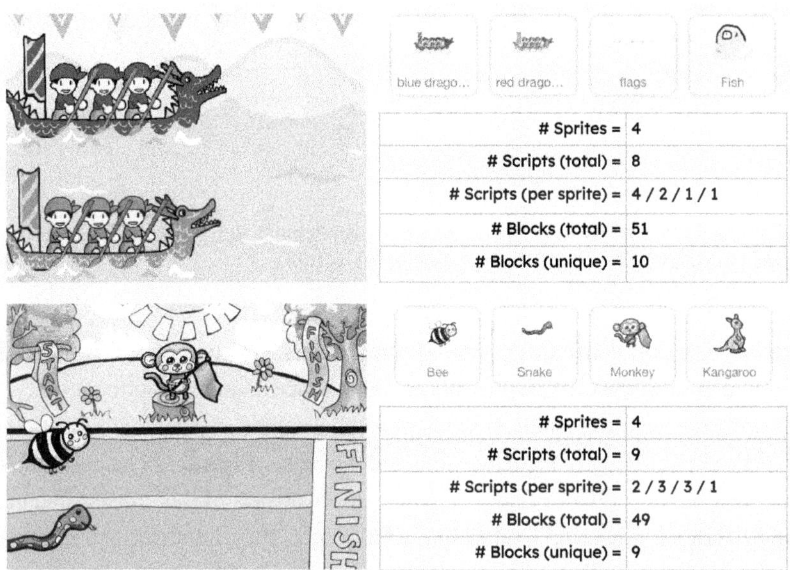

Figure 6 Examples of Scratch projects from Scratch Encore (Franklin et al. 2020). The two projects are technically similar, only differing by theme.

Large language models may also prove helpful in customizing existing assignments to an instructor's local population (creating *culturally competent projects*). Cultural competence is an aspect of culturally responsive pedagogy (CRP). It emphasizes facilitating students to honor their cultural backgrounds while developing understanding in at least one other culture through the learning materials and activities (Davis et al. 2021). At the K–8 level, the literature clearly emphasizes the value and importance of CRP (Gay 2018; Ladson-Billings 1995) and students' sense of belonging (Maslow 1958, 1962), especially in computing disciplines and among learners from under-represented groups in computing. While there are several existing culturally responsive CS curricula, a fixed set of materials will not stay responsive across time, location, and population. Thus, empowering teachers to created localized instructional materials is the next essential step.

Figure 6 presents two sample Scratch projects from the Scratch Encore curriculum (Franklin et al. 2020). The two projects are situated in different contexts/themes but teach the same CS material/concept (animating a sprite using a repeat loop with multiple costumes and, optionally, movement), largely with the same code. From the programmer's perspective, they have approximately the same number of sprites, scripts, and blocks. From the user's perspective, the projects involve one sprite animating in place (flags versus monkey), and two sprites animating across the screen (red boat and blue boat versus bee and

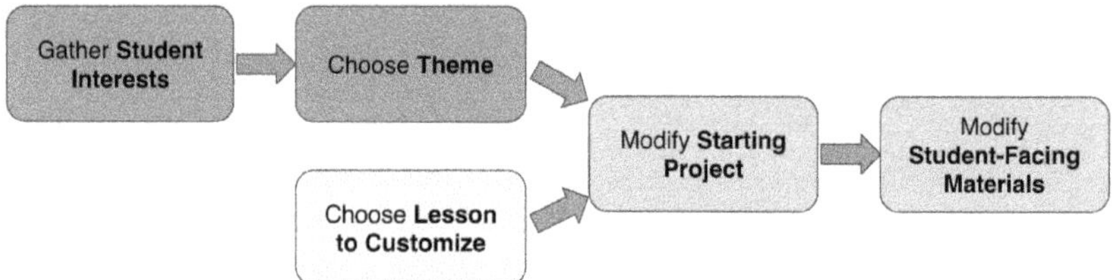

Figure 7 The steps in the process of customizing a Scratch project; adapted from Tran et al. (2024)

snake). They only differ by theme: one represents a Dragon Boat Festival race (Figure 6, top), the other represents an animal race (Figure 6, bottom).

Unfortunately, especially at the K–8 level, teachers are unlikely to have the expertise to efficiently create customized versions of lessons. The customization process is shown in Figure 7. There are two parts of the process that can be performed in parallel – choosing what project they want to customize and gathering their students' interests. The teacher can gather students' interests in many ways: via a survey, initial getting-to-know-you projects about themselves, or small group discussions with prompts. Then the teacher thinks about the attributes of the project (in this case, three sprites, two of which go across the screen left to right, and the third that animates in place) and chooses a theme that both matches the technical aspects of the sample project and will resonate with their students (especially students who might normally feel left out).

Recent work by Tran et al. (2024) explored the challenges teachers face when attempting to customize Scratch Encore lessons. Teachers were learning how to customize an existing base Scratch project as well as the corresponding student-facing worksheets. Researchers created extensive scaffolds, including instruction and a step-by-step guide for each project. The authors introduced *reskinning* – the process of modifying the visual presentation of the existing project by changing the sprites and backdrop to match with a new theme while keeping the code untouched. Using the reskinning approach, a teacher can quickly create a third, culturally competent version of the Scratch projects shown in Figure 6. They can incorporate a theme that may attract their students' attention (by changing the sprites and backdrop) while preserving the structure of the base project's code. It is critical that all existing technical attributes are followed because, for example, a project that is too easy may result in students not having sufficient knowledge to learn the next module/lesson, or a project that is too complicated may overwhelm students and cause fatigue. Even with these scaffolds, though, teachers struggled with three critical steps: (1) choosing a project that integrates the theme with the technical attributes, (2) creating

Figure 8 A query for GPT-3 to generate project ideas based on the Animal Race project from Scratch Encore. Suggested project ideas are related to the Moon Festival. The qualified idea is in green, and the disqualified idea is in red.

sprites in a timely manner (often spending too much time tweaking the figures), and (3) modifying student-facing materials.

While this reskinning approach is promising, the concern about the cognitive load on teachers and the many demands on their time, especially during the school year, remains unaddressed. Generative AI could assist with these challenges. Given the ability of LLMs to generate novel human-like text responses, Tran examined the potential of teachers using LLMs to brainstorm culturally competent Scratch project ideas (Tran 2023). The author prompted GPT-3 to suggest project ideas that technically match with a base project from Scratch Encore but related to a different theme. Their initial attempts at prompt engineering produced many positive results while also highlighting some outputs that are shallow in terms of theme. The prompt to generate project ideas for the Animation module and an example output from GPT-3 are shown in Figure 8. As we can see, the qualified project idea (in green) is in a ready-to-use state – a teacher can implement it through reskinning the Animal Race project. On the other hand, the disqualified project (in red) involves many complexity issues (e.g., a positional and timing dependency between the girl, the falling moon cakes, and the floating lanterns). In a more recent study, Tran et al. (2025) performed a systematic evaluation of 300 customized Scratch project ideas generated by GPT-3. Specifically, the authors qualitatively evaluated each generated idea for quality of theme and alignment with the base project's code and found that 81% of the generated ideas satisfied their evaluation metrics. At the same time, they identified two major shortcomings: the presence of potentially insensitive and inaccurate elements and code complexity when implementing the generated ideas in Scratch; both can be resolved with minimal modifications by teachers.

Further, text-to-image generative AI could potentially be used to generate starting sprite and backdrop images, allowing teachers to spend less time searching the internet for appropriate media. Relatively straightforward prompt engineering could be used to produce images that are suitable for Scratch: two-dimensional, cartoon-like, and with white backgrounds.

While existing research has shown the promising application of LLMs in the creation of culturally competent projects, it is critical to further approach this direction with caution due to the impressionable nature of young children and the well-documented evidence of cultural and social biases in LLM outputs (Kotek Dockum, and Sun 2023; Liang et al. 2021; Nadeem et al. 2020; Tao et al. 2024). Tran et al., in their later study (2025), have concluded that LLM-generated content is not ready as student-facing materials at the K–8 level, and emphasized the important role of teachers in performing human filtering before bringing LLM-generated materials into the classroom. Teachers should review LLM-generated content for culturally insensitive elements that do not align with their expertise, and perform a thorough content review to filter out or adjust inappropriate projects; additional training and scaffolds may be needed to support teachers in handling this.

Block-Based Code

Another potential application of LLMs at the pre-university level is in the creation of coding solutions and the evaluation of student projects, from a teacher's perspective. The major difference between the K–12 and the college settings is the use of block-based rather than text-based programming languages.

Given that block-based languages are precluded from the text-based nature of available LLM code-generation tools, researchers have attempted to use commercially available LLM models to perform two tasks: (1) creating sample solutions to block-based assignments and (2) automatically analyzing student

Scratch projects (Gonzalez-Maldonado, Liu, and Franklin 2025). To achieve that, they "trained" an existing LLM by creating two transpilers to convert Scratch code into a language that the model is more familiar with (Python and S-Expressions). Their evaluation of the LLM performance on both tasks indicated that prompt engineering alone is insufficient to guide the model to reliably produce high-quality outputs. For projects of medium complexity, the LLM consistently generated solutions that do not follow correct block-based syntax or only produced correct solutions in a few instances with correct syntax. In terms of analyzing student code, the study found a correlation between scores assigned by an existing auto-grader and those assigned by the LLM, but there remained great discrepancies between the "actual" scores and the LLM-generated scores. While current LLM models, without fine-tuning, are not ready to use for block-based programming class preparation, this study provides valuable insights into this novel application of LLMs in K–12 CS education.

4.5 Assessment Questions

Creating equivalent problems is not only useful for cultural competence. It also provides a solution for running testing facilities at scale as university class sizes grow.

There is a desire to have live coding exercises during exams. Allowing students to use their own devices can be challenging, because it may be impossible to monitor their use of the internet to look up references or even solutions to the exam questions. On the other hand, testing facilities large enough to support a multi-hundred-student exam can be prohibitively expensive. Fowler et al. (2024) studied dynamically creating equivalent coding problems so that a single computer lab could be used for a class of students, with each student making an appointment for their exam. Since the questions are dynamically generated (with constraints), reporting exact questions to others is unlikely to give them a significant advantage. In this work, the authors chose very specific problem types (e.g., find the largest element in an array) and determined which other closely related, but not identical, problems (e.g., find the smallest element in an array) were of equivalent difficulty. Once a single problem has enough variations, then it can be put into the bank, and one of the variations is chosen at the moment of the exam.

The process of creating and validating identical problems with slight technical variations is very time consuming, and the authors of the previous study did not utilize generative AI. Instead, they analyzed common problem types and hand-coded the transformation that generated different versions of the problem from one starting problem.

One potential approach would therefore be to leverage the work tailoring programming exercises to individual interests (Del Carpio Gutierrez et al. 2024; Leinonen et al. 2021) to assessment questions in order to mask the fact that the problems are technically identical. Such an approach, once validated on a subset, could lead to a much higher variety of potentially equivalent problems. Hand-coding each different possibility would be prohibitive, but using generative AI would provide a wealth of creative, interesting problems very quickly, even on demand.

5 Class Instruction

Generative AI can also be used to provide help directly to learners in ways that enhance learning. As class sizes increase, the opportunities students have for synchronous help from instructional staff decrease.

The integration of AI directly into development environments, and as digital teaching assistants (Hicke et al. 2023), represents a significant shift in educational support. Such tools can provide instant and personalized support outside the traditional classroom setting. Furthermore, the adaptation of curricula and teaching materials, including innovative textbooks like that of Porter and Zingaro (2023), which teaches Python programming using tools like Copilot and ChatGPT, illustrates the evolving nature of educational delivery. The advent of generative AI in computing education represents both a challenge and an opportunity. Educators are tasked with integrating these technologies into the curriculum in a way that enhances learning while preparing students for a future where AI is a fundamental aspect of problem-solving.

In this section, we first explore how current class instruction can be enhanced through generative AI tools. We divide this discussion into two types. First, we consider ways a student, on their own, could use generative AI to assist in tasks they have traditionally completed on their own. Next, we consider instances where they would traditionally reach out to instructional staff (when they are stuck). We recognize that this is not a hard and fast line; it is merely a way of organizing the many ideas on how to leverage generative AI technology. Finally, we explore a more transformative idea, in which generative AI is provided more autonomy in directing the learning process.

5.1 Student Resources

Explaining example code

While textbooks provide high-quality instruction, students supplement formal instruction with searches on the internet. The code they find online may be related to the topic, but it may be poorly documented, and include neither a high-level explanation nor line-by-line comments. The same approach that was previously described to generate explanations for online textbooks could also be used directly by students to enhance the learning potential of code found on the internet.

Explaining Concepts

Analogies can be a particularly effective type of explanation, as they help students bridge the gap between existing knowledge and unfamiliar concepts. The flexibility of LLMs has shown they are capable of generating cross-domain analogies which could be applied in a range of creative contexts (Ding et al. 2023). This is especially important in educational contexts, given that creating effective educational analogies is difficult even for experienced instructors.

Bernstein et al. (2024) explored this idea in an introductory programming context by having students generate analogies for understanding recursion, a particularly challenging threshold concept in computer science (Sanders and McCartney 2016). Their study involved 385 first-year students who were asked to generate their own analogies using ChatGPT. The students were provided a code snippet and were tasked with creating recursion-based analogies, optionally including personally relevant topics in their prompts. A wide range of topics were specified by students, including common topics such as cooking, books, and sports, which also appeared in ChatGPT-generated analogies when a topic was not specified. Other topics specified by students, such as video games and board games, were not present in the themes that were generated by ChatGPT. This suggests that while LLMs can generate bespoke analogies on-demand, students may benefit from being "in-the-loop", as the inclusion of their personal interests and experiences can lead to more diverse and engaging analogies. Students reported enjoying the activity and indicated that the generated analogies improved their understanding and retention of recursion. This approach underscores how generative AI can be leveraged in computing education: not just as a tool for generating explanations, but as a means of empowering students to create their own, tailored learning resources.

5.2 Assignment Assistance

With respect to assignment assistance, we consider two aspects: how the feedback is delivered and what kind is required.

Providing feedback is critical for student learning. Research on best practices for feedback show that the most effective feedback is specific (Hattie and Timperley 2007), timely (Opitz, Ferdinand, and Mecklinger 2011), aligned toward a student goal (Hattie and Timperley 2007), and surprising (Malone 1981).

In addition, it is helpful to think about several different types of help a student might need (Franklin et al. 2013), beyond "help me finish this assignment." Some students merely need confirmation they are on the right track, especially if they are not confident in their abilities. Others need just a reminder of a keyword or concept, allowing them to look at their notes or elsewhere to put that concept into practice. Some students know what concept to use but have a small conceptual barrier that needs to be resolved before they can move on. Finally, some may need to have an entire set of concepts retaught to them.

With synchronous, interactive support, a human teaching assistant can provide the right level of help – asking a series of probing questions to hone in on the topic and on the level of help the learner needs. However, in large classes, human TAs may not always be available, with scheduled office hours at inconvenient times for some learners or not fully used when they are offered (M. Smith et al. 2017). Face-to-face support also doesn't always serve all students fairly, with some students reluctant to ask for help, while others may dominate the available time (A. J. Smith et al. 2017).

Automated feedback can be provided in several ways. For each general mechanism, we first consider how assistance has been provided as class sizes have increased, prior to LLMs. We then present several projects that have evaluated LLMs for providing help to students. It is important to note that LLM technology has been improving rapidly – a technique evaluated just two years ago may be much more successful today.

Discussion Boards

A discussion board is an online forum where students can ask questions of the entire class or just to the instructional staff. While neither synchronous nor interactive, a discussion board has two main benefits. First, peers can answer each others' questions, lowering the burden for instructional staff and providing potentially faster responses. Second, students can look at previous posts and find answers to their questions without needing to ask.

Prior research analyzing student use of a discussion board examined posts from 395 students across two courses, revealing three major results (Vellukunnel et al. 2017). First, many posts related to logistical or relatively shallow questions. This is positive, because the discussion relieved instructional staff of the burden of answering simple questions while allowing in-person office hours to focus more on deep questions related to understanding. Second, the largest portion of questions reflected some level of constructive problem-solving activity, indicating that students were receiving substantive help. Finally, asking questions on the forum was positively correlated with course grades. The study did not, however, answer questions about whether the time instructional staff spent answering questions was lower than without the forum, nor whether peers provided high-quality assistance.

Early work proposed an automated discussion-bot that would answer student questions on discussion forums (Feng et al. 2006). Instead of using a large language model trained on vast amounts of data on the internet, the bot used information retrieval and natural language processing techniques to mine answers from an annotated corpus of 1236 archived discussions and 279 course documents. They tested their bot with 66 questions, finding only 14 answers were determined to be exactly correct, whereas half were considered "good answers."

More recently, the use of LLMs to assist with discussion forums has been explored (Zhang et al. 2023). The authors used an LLM to classify questions as conceptual, homework, logistics, and not answerable (by the LLM). Using GPT-3, they achieved 81% classification accuracy overall, extending to 93% accuracy for classifying unanswerable questions, meaning the approach can effectively ignore questions that it cannot answer, which could reduce the occurrence of unhelpful responses or hallucinations.

Liu and M'Hiri (2024) took this one step further by simulating an LLM-powered teaching assistant on questions collected from the discussion board of a massive introductory programming course. Using LLM chains – a prompt engineering technique where several different prompts iteratively build toward a final solution: the first prompt classifies the question being answered, then uses that classification to inform what model/parameters/prompt to use to generate a candidate answer. Another prompt then assesses the quality of the answer. The authors ran a series of student questions through the model and found that the LLM-powered virtual TA:

- was proficient at categorizing questions as either homework questions, coding feedback requests, or explanation requests;
- provided more detailed responses than those provided by the human TAs;
- matched the accuracy of TA responses with regard to non-assignment-specific questions;
- had a tendency to include an overwhelming amount of information.

They concluded that while their findings are promising, human oversight is still required.

Automated Test Suites and Feedback

Another automated approach is to provide a test suite that generates feedback for students in the form of which tests their solution passed and failed. While this is useful in supporting students in some ways, creating test cases is a critical skill, both for test-driven development[2] and debugging. In test-driven development, test cases are created *before* the main code in order to help the programmer test code as it is developed. It can also be a useful metacognitive technique to help students form a correct mental model of the problem they are working on. One study found that students in an intervention group that created test cases prior to coding exhibited similar completion rates as the control group but with significantly fewer errors related to incorrect mental models (Denny et al. 2019). This provides support for the design decision in 2005 for Web-CAT (a popular automated assessment tool) to support student submission of test cases in addition to their solution code (Allowatt and Edwards 2005).

The advantage of automated test suites, with respect to the features of effective feedback, is that it is timely. The responses are often nearly instantaneous. Unfortunately though, the form of the feedback is nonspecific and the information returned can vary greatly. The least information that could be provided would be just a final numeric score, giving the student an indication of how correct their code is. Other instructors may provide information about every test case, highlighting which ones failed (e.g., the test inputs and desired outputs). While this allows the student to start debugging on their own, it has been shown to encourage students to "debug their program into existence" whereby students lose track of the learning goals and focus exclusively on passing the automated test-cases (Zamprogno, Holmes, and Baniassad 2020).

In practice, however, students are unlikely to have automated suites that provide them a numerical quality score when developing code in the real world. LLMs have the potential to unlock an entirely new type of automated feedback that more closely aligns with real-world coding practices. They can provide students with suggested code edits/next steps, meaningful feedback on code readability, efficiency, and design patterns. This type of feedback, which is often overlooked in traditional education settings where class sizes commonly reach hundreds of students, can help bridge the gap between academic learning and industry practices.

Nguyen and Allan (2024) explored the potential of generating this type of 'formative' feedback using LLMs. The authors used GPT-4 and "few-shot learning" – providing the model with some examples of the expected input and output within the prompt – to generate individualized feedback for 113 student submissions. They prompted the model to generate feedback on the student's

---

[2] Test-driven development is a software development practice that focuses on creating unit test cases before developing the actual code. It is an iterative approach combining programming, unit test creation, and refactoring.

conceptual understanding, syntax, and time complexity and also had the model generate guiding questions or suggest follow-up actions. The group found that the feedback provided by the LLM was generally correct. The model provided correct evaluations of conceptual understanding for 92% of the submissions, syntax for 89% of submissions, and time complexity for 90% of submissions. The model was also found to be useful at generating code suggestions and hints (92% of submissions received code suggestions that were at least "somewhat correct" and 95% of hints were conceptually correct). Despite these promising results, the authors also identified several issues including a significant difference in model performance across different programming assignments and a tendency for GPT's suggestions to lead to a suboptimal solution.

Code Explanations

We previously discussed using LLMs to generate code explanations for textbooks (MacNeil et al. 2023, Leinonen, Denny, et al. 2023). One intriguing possibility is to leverage this same functionality to generate explanations of a student's own code in order to help them understand and debug code they have written.

Balse et al. (2023) used an LLM, specifically GPT-3.5-turbo, to generate explanations for logical errors in code written by students in an introductory programming course (CS1). The authors aimed to determine if LLM-generated explanations could support teaching assistants (TAs) in providing feedback to students efficiently. The quality of LLM-generated explanations was evaluated in two ways: the TA's perception of explanation quality (comparing LLM-generated to peer-generated) and a detailed manual analysis of the LLM-generated explanations for all selected buggy student solutions. They found that TAs rated the quality of LLM-generated explanations comparably to peer-generated explanations. However, a manual analysis revealed that 50% of LLM explanations contained at least one incorrect statement, although 93% correctly identified at least one logical error.

Synchronous Assistance

LLMs show great promise for providing on-demand help at a large scale, especially if they can be designed to respond to student queries in a similar way to trained teaching assistants. This idea has been of significant interest in the computing education community.

Liffiton et al. (2024) describe a novel tool called "CodeHelp", which incorporates "guardrails" to avoid directly revealing solutions. Deployed in a first-year computer and data science course, the tool's effectiveness, student usage patterns, and perceptions were analyzed over a 12-week period. Rather than replacing existing instructional support, the goal of the work was to complement educator help by offloading simple tasks and being available at times that would inconvenient for the teacher or teaching assistants.

CodeHelp was well received by both students and instructors for its availability and assistance with debugging, although challenges included ensuring relevancy and appropriateness of the AI-generated responses and preventing over-reliance. A follow-up study by Sheese et al. (2024), investigated students' patterns of help-seeking when utilizing CodeHelp, analysing more than 2,500 student queries. The study involved manual categorization of the queries into the types of assistance sought (e.g., debugging, implementation, conceptual understanding), alongside automated analysis of query characteristics (e.g., information provided by students). The authors found that the majority of queries were seeking immediate help with programming assignments rather than focusing on in-depth conceptual understanding. In addition, students often provided minimal information in their queries, pointing to a need for further instruction on how to effectively communicate with the tool.

Yang et al. (2024) further expanded on this work by conducting think-aloud sessions aimed at exploring student help-seeking behaviors during the debugging process. They developed the "CS50 Duck" chatbot, a "pedagogically-minded subject-matter expert that guides students towards solutions and fosters learning." Notably the CS50 Duck made use of retrieval-augmented generation (RAG) in order to pull information from a "ground truth" database of lecture captions so as to ensure responses were correct and more relevant to the content covered by the specific course. The authors identified several broad categories of help-seeking behavior that students exhibited when interacting with their chatbot:

- *Code Comprehension* Instances where a student asked the chatbot to explain a snippet of code or its expected output
- *Error Comprehension* Asking for a plain English explanation of an error message, for example: *What is a segmentation fault?*
- *Hypothesis Testing* When a student inquires about methods to test a hypothesis regarding the location or cause of a bug
- *Implementing a Solution* Asking for the proper code or syntax to fix an identified bug
- *Broad Debugging Question* Providing code to the chatbot and asking it to identify and/or solve the bug

The authors observed that student help-seeking behaviors were not novel or unique but corresponded with previously identified web-search debugging behaviors such as using Stack Overflow to test a hypothesis. Crucially, the authors noted that while the students found the chatbot to be a helpful source of domain and experiential knowledge, they did not perceive it as a primary source for learning debugging *strategies*, choosing instead to rely on human tutors (TAs, instructors, peers, etc.) for strategic and procedural knowledge.

Recent research focusing on the desirable characteristics for AI teaching assistants in programming courses highlighted the importance of supporting meaningful learning experiences rather than simply providing direct answers (Denny, MacNeil et al., 2024). The authors found that students value digital TAs that offer instant, engaging support, particularly around peak times such as before assessment deadlines. Key characteristics identified by students include the ability of the AI to scaffold learning by guiding them through problem-solving steps and providing explanations rather than direct solutions. Moreover, students emphasized the importance of maintaining their autonomy during the learning process, preferring tools that encourage them to develop their own solutions rather than becoming overly dependent on the assistant.

5.2.1 Assessing Student Learning

Large language models may make grading less time-consuming, permitting the use of question types that are under-utilized due to difficulties in grading in large classes. For example, despite the widely acknowledged value of Explain in Plain English questions for developing code comprehension, the difficulty in grading students' subjective responses makes them infeasible for large class sizes. A typical EiPE question presents a student with a small fragment of code, and the task for the student is to explain the purpose of the code fragment in abstract terms.

Smith et al. (2023) describe an innovative approach for grading EiPE questions using large language models, whereby the student reads and attempts to understand a shown fragment of code, and then crafts an explanation in natural language. This explanation is then provided as the input prompt to a code-generating LLM, and the code that is generated is automatically tested for equivalence with the original code using a test suite. Denny et al. evaluate this approach, as illustrated in Figure 9, in an introductory programming course with approximately 900 students (Denny, Smith et al. 2024; D. H. Smith, Denny, and Fowler 2024). They analysed success rates and prompt lengths, and classified prompts according to the Structure of Observed Learning Outcomes (SOLO) taxonomy (Lister et al. 2006). Student perceptions of these tasks were also gathered through surveys and thematic analysis to understand their views on the educational validity of using LLMs for assessing code comprehension.

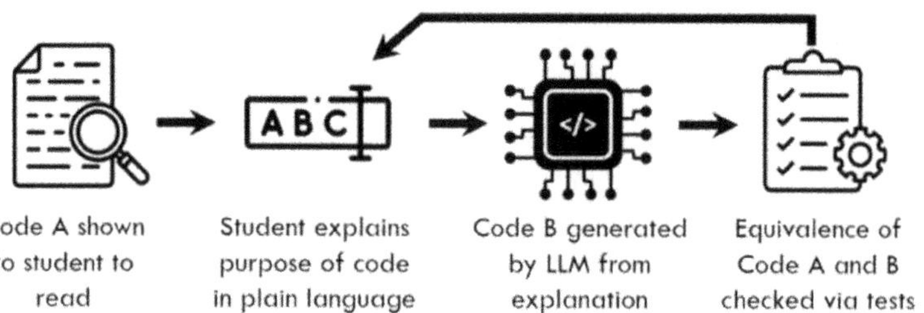

Figure 9 Using an LLM to provide automated feedback on "Explain in plain English" tasks, as described by Denny, Smith et al. (2024)

Students were largely successful in crafting prompts that led to code being generated that was functionally equivalent to the code they were asked to explain. Relational responses, which demonstrate a high-level understanding of the purpose of a code fragment, were most likely to result in correct code generation. The study noted a positive correlation between the success of student prompts and their classification within the higher categories of the SOLO taxonomy.

Student feedback revealed that they found the activity engaging and believed it enhanced their code comprehension skills. However, some expressed concerns about the effectiveness of this pedagogical approach for more complex coding tasks and its comparison to traditional coding practices. The authors recommended that educators balance prompt writing exercises with more traditional coding exercises to cover a broader spectrum of learning objectives, including the development of programming skills for more complex tasks. However, this study demonstrates the potential of LLMs as a tool for both teaching and assessing programming skills.

6 Designing for the User

We have reviewed a number of independent, separate ways that LLMs can be used to provide support for a variety of preparation and teaching tasks. These have tended to focus on the technical point of view – in other words, what LLMs are *capable of.* However, each research paper we reviewed may have involved many hours of prompt engineering to determine how to create a consistent prompt that provides the best possible results. Some tasks may not need a great deal of engineering, whereas others, like the work to generate ideas for themed Scratch projects, take a substantial amount of time to produce responses that contain accurate and complete information.

This section discusses how LLM-powered tools should be presented to the user. We present three examples: one that exists and two that are the focus of future work.

6.1 Preparatory Materials

In Section 4, we described different ways LLMs could help teachers create materials for their classrooms. What should this process look like from the educator's perspective? Let's consider creating assignments. As described in the process of customizing a Scratch project, we will assume that educators are starting from a curriculum. Given an assignment, perhaps they want a technically equivalent assignment with a creative scenario / theme. Thus, the LLM needs two pieces of information: the original assignment and the desired theme. However, with integration, the LLM can also generate themes.

There is growing interest in how to design user interfaces for educational applications that incorporate generative AI, especially for users with little technical experience. Recently, Pozdniakov et al. (2024) proposed a framework for user-centric applications to make generative AI more accessible and effective in educational settings. One significant design decision is how much autonomy to give the educator and how much to abstract away. Let's consider the scenario in which a K–8 teacher, perhaps without a computer science degree and limited experience working with generative AI tools, wants help creating a project. We could create a system that integrates all of the steps, providing support and guidance throughout the process.

Figure 10 depicts such a system. Each box represents a phase that is an interactive step with a specific prompt for a generative AI tool, and the output is next to it. We now describe the different steps, what the interface would be for the teacher, and how we balance teacher agency and control with hiding the technical details. The figure depicts the customization of a single project, drawn from the Animation Module of the Scratch Encore curriculum. The information for the Animation Module has already been encoded in the system – including the prompt from Figure 8 and the original project code.

Brainstorm Themes We first assist the teacher in brainstorming possible themes. We ask the teacher a variety of questions about their classrooms, including the countries their students come from, the town and state of their

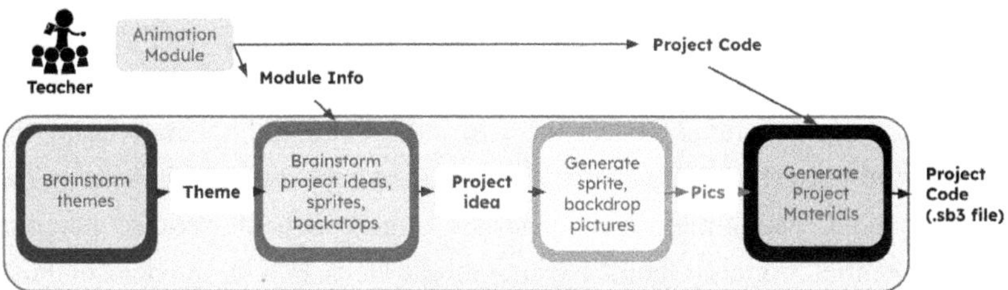

Figure 10 The generative AI-assisted workflow of an integrated tool to help K–8 teachers create customized Scratch projects

school, local events that occur, and school-based events. We have prompts for each of these pieces of information on which to generate new ideas. The teacher may be presented with around 10–15 ideas from which to choose. The teacher can then choose one of the suggested themes or can use one of their own. The information from the teacher can be saved so that if they want to customize a different project, the system already has information about their environment. All details of the prompts are hidden, and the agency we provide the teacher is to be able to choose none of the suggested themes and enter their own.

Brainstorm Project Ideas The specific project ideas are a combination of the technical attributes of the original project and the theme the teacher chose. Using the prompts from Figure 8, we use an LLM to provide four suggestions to the teacher, each identifying the background, each sprite, and a sentence or two about what is occurring in the project. The teacher is allowed to edit aspects of any of the suggested ideas or to specify their own idea in the provided format. The format is critical because the different elements will be taken from the entry and used by the next step to generate sprite and backdrop pictures.

Generate Sprite and Backdrop Pictures The next step is to create pictures for the teacher. There are three potential mechanisms for obtaining images. First, we can draw upon the Scratch sprite library, which is freely available for all Scratch projects. Second, we can generate a few suggestions from a generative AI image generator such as DALL-E. Finally, we can give the teacher more agency to enter more specific attributes for the pictures. A first attempt would be to provide, as a default, a combination of Scratch images and images from our prompt. Our prompt is a combination of the attributes described from the project idea stage and characteristics that we have found generate more appropriate images (e.g., specifying different skin colors to highlight diversity, asking for 2-d cartoony images, and asking for a white background). Finally, we could give the teacher more agency – the question is how much? We could expose the prompt to them so they could directly edit it, or we could provide a user interface asking more questions about the attributes they want (potentially choosing clothing and skin color for a person). At the end of this stage, the system would have the images for sprites and backgrounds.

Generate Project Materials The final step, integrating sprites into the projects and student-facing materials, could be coded, though not through generative AI. Because we have starting documents, the new images could replace the old images, providing the teachers with a draft of their final materials. Generating the project code is straightforward, just replacing the images in the original file. Creating the project materials is more difficult because there are many potential formats (Google Forms, Google Docs, PDFs), and none of those are stored in a public format that is easy to automatically manipulate.

When this process is complete, there would still be work for the teacher to do. The images may not be the same size as the original ones, so the teacher may need to change the default sizes. In addition, the starting position and exact movements might be different in the new project, so teachers could adjust those. However, it would greatly reduce the amount of time teachers require to create such projects.

6.2 Integrated Development Environments (IDE)

Integrated development environments (IDEs) in educational settings are designed to provide students with a supportive platform for coding and testing their solutions. Research has explored the direct integration of code-generating LLMs within IDEs. Kazemitabaar et al. (2023) explored the impact of providing OpenAI Codex to novice learners in an introductory programming context. They conducted a controlled experiment involving participants aged 10–17 who had no prior text-based programming experience. Participants were divided into two groups; one had access to Codex directly integrated into the programming environment, and the other did not. All participants completed a set of Python code-authoring tasks, followed by code-modification tasks.

They found that the use of Codex significantly improved code-authoring performance, with no negative impacts on manual code modification tasks. Interestingly, learners with prior programming competency (as determined by Scratch pretest scores) benefitted more from having access to the AI code generator, as measured by performance on retention tests. However, there were concerns about potential over-reliance on AI-generated code, given that when code was generated by the AI model, around half of the time it was submitted by students without them making any changes to it.

Although the integration of tools like GitHub Copilot into IDEs has shown promise, these tools were primarily designed with experienced programmers in mind. Their current design often assumes a level of proficiency that many novices do not yet possess, which may lead to frustration or confusing experiences for beginners. The adaptation of these tools to better suit the needs of novice programmers is therefore essential.

Prather, Reeves, et al. (2023) have outlined a comprehensive set of design implications that address this concern, proposing several enhancements to make these tools more novice-friendly. One of the key issues identified is that novices can become easily distracted or overwhelmed by immediately generated and displayed code suggestions, especially when these suggestions consist of multiple lines of code. This often leads to an increased cognitive load, as students struggle to make sense of the suggestions while simultaneously trying to learn the underlying concepts. To mitigate this, Prather et al. argue that there should be a mechanism that allows students to have greater control over the kinds of suggestions they receive and when those suggestions are presented. For example, students could benefit from a feature that enables them to request help only when they feel it is necessary, rather than being presented with suggestions unsolicited in real time.

Other design implications identified by Prather et al. highlight the importance of integrating metacognitive scaffolding into these tools. These could involve special UI elements that guide students through problem-solving steps or provide a clearer understanding of alternative solutions. Additionally, improving the design of these tools to help students build better mental models is another important implication. Many novices struggle to understand how and why certain code is generated by tools like Copilot. Incorporating elements of Explainable AI (XAI) into these systems, where the reasoning behind code suggestions is made transparent, could help students to develop a deeper understanding of the logic and structure of the code they are working with.

There has also been work done to enhance the development environment of students by using LLMs to provide plain-English explanations of syntax and compilation errors. A common grievance among novice programmers is the frustration and confusion caused by ambiguous or obtuse error messages produced by their programming environments with something as simple as a missing brace sometimes producing a long and complex error message. By leveraging the ability of LLMs to understand and translate computer programs, these environments can significantly reduce the cognitive load on students, making it easier for them to focus on the fundamental concepts being taught rather than deciphering complex error messages.

In early work, Leinonen, Hellas et al. (2023) studied the ability of the Codex model to explain some Python error messages commonly perceived as having poor readability for novices (for example, "can't assign function call", "invalid token", "illegal target for annotation", "EOL while scanning string literal", "unicode error") and found that most of the explanations generated were considered comprehensible by the two researchers tasked with evaluating the explanations. Codex was likewise able to provide a correct fix to the underlying error 33% of the time. The authors noted great variability in the quality of explanations with regard to different types of error messages.

More recently Taylor et al. (2024) incorporated LLM error explanations into the Debugging C Compiler (dcc) and evaluated it at the CS1 and CS2 level. The Debugging C Compiler is a C/C++ compiler aimed at providing novice students with additional scaffolding when developing their programs.

The compiler embeds run-time error detection tools (i.e., Valgrind, Address-Sanitizer, and GDB) into the executables it compiles so as to provide additional error explanations such as stack printouts and has enhanced, hand-crafted explanations for a range of common errors. For their study the authors created the 'dcc –help' command which uses gpt-3.5-turbo-0301 to "consume source code, error messages, and locations to generate contextual, novice-friendly error and warning explanations designed to augment typical compiler output." The authors evaluated the LLM enhanced help messages by collecting 400 error/explanation pairs (200 compile time errors and 200 runtime errors) generated by students enrolled in their institution's CS1/2 courses and evaluated each pair for conceptual accuracy, correctness, relevance, and completeness. Additionally, the authors evaluated whether the generated response's overall quality would be commensurate to that of either a peer or a tutor. The study found that the LLM-generated explanations for compile-time errors consistently outperformed those for runtime errors. Specifically, compile-time explanations were considered conceptually accurate 90% of the time while only 75% of runtime error explanations were conceptually accurate. With regard to correctness the authors found that 90% of compile-time explanations were correct versus 66% of runtime error explanations. The authors also found compile-time explanations to be more relevant (92% relevancy vs. 75%) and complete (72% vs. 39%) than runtime explanations. Similarly 72% of compile-time explanations were found to be of "tutor" quality compared to only 45% of runtime explanations.

6.3 Personalized Tutors

In Ender's Game, a book by Orson Scott Card, the main character, Ender, has an AI-powered tutor throughout his life. While computer science education is not training a child to save his species, the characteristics of this tutor are intriguing. It had full autonomy to pose problems and have discussions with Ender. It is worth exploring what research has been done toward this end and where generative AI may fit in.

However, we want to make it clear that in this discussion, we are not proposing that we replace teachers with a computer. We believe that teachers are incredibly valuable, and no computer will be able to replace many of the attributes that teachers have. Studies on infants and toddlers have shown that babies do not learn as well from people in videos speaking to them compared to when their in-person caretakers speak to them, even when they use the same words and way of speaking. While we can talk about technical capabilities, we do not fully understand the emotional aspects of learning, and that is just as or more important than the technical aspects.

Intelligent Tutoring Systems (ITS) have been researched for decades; however, discussion of their use has sometimes been controversial because (a) some have proposed them as teacher replacements, not fully respecting and acknowledging the unique, important attributes that teachers have, (b) they have always fallen far short of the lofty, unrealistic goal of being a full tutor, and (c) the time required to create the question bank, associated feedback, and decision mechanisms about how quickly / when to increase difficulty is tremendously time consuming and expensive. Despite these drawbacks, they still have made major contributions to automated, personalized education, so they must be acknowledged as relevant pre-generative AI prior work.

Intelligent tutors have two distinct roles. First, they use a learner's performance on previous problems to determine the next problem they will be asked to solve. Second, they provide instruction / help / feedback to solve the current problem. ITSs are widely available, and they are used in both formal education and informal education, primarily for mathematics and language subjects.

School homework They can be assigned for homework while learning math facts, such as memorization of basic addition, subtraction, multiplication, and division facts. The ITS quizzes the learner on simpler problems first, and for any answers they get wrong, they provide the answer and then quiz them more often on similar problems. Eventually, learners show mastery, and the ITS moves on to slightly harder problems.

Informal math learning In the informal space, there are apps such as Prodigy,[3] in which the user is a character in an adventure game in which they explore different places, go on quests, and fight monsters. The battles all involve solving a math question to power their attacks. Like the math facts system, the system repeats the same level of question when the player gets it wrong and advances the level when they show mastery. However, it has extensive content, far beyond memorization of math facts.

Informal language learning A widely popular application for learning languages is Duolingo,[4] which has millions of informal users. Not only does it dynamically determine what questions to give based on user mistakes, it has integrated an extensive feedback and reward system. If a user gets the same type of question wrong enough times, it provides instruction (such as presenting a conjugation rule and a few examples). The reward system is especially extensive. There is a streak that is maintained by completing at least one lesson per day. In addition, completing any lesson in the morning triggers a double bonus for 15 minutes if someone completes a lesson in the evening, and vice versa.

---

[3] www.prodigygame.com/main-en/
[4] www.duolingo.com/learn

Therefore, if someone spends 15 minutes each morning and evening on the system, their points increase dramatically. Points are used to advance in "leagues" in which users compete with strangers in the same league to attempt to gain the most points each week.

Supporting Computer Science ITS Development There have been ITSs created for teaching coding, but their quality varies (Crow, Luxton-Reilly, and Wuensche 2018), and none are in widespread use. Generative AI could be used to support many of the steps of development for a coding-based ITS. The following steps would need to be required to create an ITS for computer science:

- ITS questions are usually small enough that they can be answered in less than a minute, whereas many computer science assignments and exercises typically take several minutes to a few hours. Therefore, one first step would be to create problem types that can be ***solved quickly*** *and lead to learning that can be applied to larger problems*. Gen AI can be used to synthesize problems of various types, including Parsons problems, code-tracing problems, and code-explanation problems, all of which can be solved quickly with rapid feedback, making them suitable for integration into an ITS.

- ***Large question banks*** need to be created, organized into equivalence classes of difficulty and concepts covered, and have gradual mechanisms for increasing difficulty. Given a single question, GenAI can be used to create many different, equivalent questions to populate this question bank.

- ***Feedback and explanations*** need to be created and tied to sets of questions. There has been significant research on using GenAI to create feedback and explanations.

- The system would need to be tuned to provide an ***optimal path of efficient, effective learning***. Too many questions at a similar level may cause learners to spend too much time in the system or lose motivation, but advancing too quickly would leave them confused. The questions need to fit within a learner's zone of proximal development (ZPD), which refers to the range of tasks that a learner can perform with guidance but cannot yet perform independently.

7 Challenges Posed by Learners' Misuse of Generative AI

While AI code generators are a new technology, code plagiarism is certainly not a new problem in introductory computer science classes. Prior to the internet, common approaches to cheating in coursework included copying solutions from another student (whether through collusion or without the other student's knowledge) and obtaining solutions from an external party, such as an organization or archive that collected prior student work (e.g., some fraternities and sororities maintained such collections).

Once the internet came into widespread use, solutions to common programming problems became readily available online. One of the reasons LLMs are so capable at solving basic programming tasks is because countless examples of solutions to these tasks are widely available on the internet. The proliferation of websites designed to teach programming as well as people posting solutions to common coding problems has made finding code to canonical programming problems trivially easy.

More recently, the scaling of the size of introductory programming courses and the availability of online grading platforms has changed the way students complete coding assignments and assessments in some universities. Online systems can provide instant feedback, supporting students in an era of small instructional staff-to-student ratios. Online assessments can be graded automatically, reducing the grading burden on instructional staff. Few universities, however, have the facilities for an entire multi-hundred-student class to take a coding examination at the same time on university computers, so students may take the exam at different times, increasing the probability of students finding out exam questions prior to their taking the exam.

The other consideration is GenAI's ability to generate code accurately. As discussed in Section 2, Gen AI is producing increasingly accurate, though not perfect, code for typical introductory coding courses. Therefore, we will focus our discussion on coding problems at this level of difficulty.

The level of alarm with the introduction of LLMs is very high, as if it is a new technology that will greatly increase the amount of plagiarism, and therefore learning loss, of introductory students. However, it would be useful to understand to what degree there is an *increase* in such behaviors compared to before. Cheating, in general, is widespread – 65–75% of undergrads admit to cheating at least one time, and 19–20% admit to cheating at least five times. Studies have found that student cheating has increased dramatically in the last 30 years (McCabe et al. 2001).

Prior to GenAI, one study analyzed patterns of plagiarism in coding courses and the effects on learning (Pierce and Zilles 2017). They had a number of interesting findings. First, the majority of plagiarism identified was between semesters (57%) rather than within a semester (43%). Second, the majority of plagiarism was by students who only plagiarized once; 64% cheated once, 19% twice, 10% three times, and 5% four times. Third, plagiarism did lead to learning loss; while plagiarized assignments earned higher grades on that assignment, those students scored marginally lower on assessments (0.89

points on a 0–12 point scale). The differences were found to be statistically significant (p = 0.00019).

A newer study has attempted to quantify both the increase in cheating and the effects on learning as a result of the advent of GenAI (B. Chen et al. 2024). They used a variety of sources of information to conclude that the quantity of cheating has increased. First, the difference in scores between unproctored quizzes and proctored exams has increased by a statistically significant amount ($p < 0.001$). Second, a larger proportion of students have plagiarism indicators present in their coding assignments. They calculate a *plagiarism ratio* to capture the percentage of assignments each student has plagiarized, and conclude that the learning loss due to plagiarism has increased.

In this section, we consider three separate aspects of misuse – detection, learning impacts, and assignment design. For each element, we first present techniques already developed to address unauthorized use of others' solutions – either from the internet or from peers. Then we consider any additional challenges that LLMs may pose.

7.1 Detecting Unauthorized Use

Perhaps the most commonly used tool to detect plagiarism in computing education is MOSS (Measure of Software Similarity). Developed in 1994 by Alex Aiken (Alex Aiken (n.d.)), MOSS is a tool that compares multiple student submissions to identify similarities between pairs of programs. Unlike a simple text comparison, MOSS uses a technique called winnowing, which generates fingerprints of the code by analyzing overlapping chunks of text (called k-grams) and selecting key features for comparison. This method allows MOSS to detect similarities even when variable and function names have been changed or comments have been rewritten, which are common techniques students use to obscure plagiarism. By focusing on the structure and logic of the code rather than the surface details, MOSS provides a robust way to identify unauthorized reuse of code.

A more recent detector, Algae, was created for detecting cheating in the previously described study (Pierce and Zilles 2017). It has several different detectors that separately detect common cheating patterns. Each detector performs a set of transformations to remove superficial differences from code and hash the result using SHA-256 to generate a single number for each file. Any two files with the same number are considered identical.

- **Near-Identical (Lazy)** This performs a simpler method than MOSS. It converts all text to uppercase and removes all comments, whitespace, and some extraneous punctuation.

- **Identical Token Stream (IdentToken)** first performs Lazy transformations, then performs additional transformations so that unique names, such as variable names, are ignored.
- **Modified Token Edit Distance (MTED)** first performs IdentToken transformations, then it reorders functions by number of tokens and only analyzes code within functions.
- **Inverted Token Index (InvToken)** first performs IdentToken transformations, but it looks for matching substrings rather than identical token streams. It then weights the identical substrings it finds. InvToken is the detector that is the most similar to MOSS.
- **Inverted Identifier Index (InvIdents)** searches for similar, unique variable and function names. All names are converted to lower case, underscores removed, and written to a file. It then looks for the most similar files.
- **Statistical Individual Dissimilarity (Obfuscation)** looks for the indicators of software obfuscation tools. It collects information such as the length of the longest line, average identifier length, number of lines, and other metrics. For each statistic, the mean and standard deviation are computed, and a submission is flagged if its sum of the absolute value of the z-scores for each statistic exceeds a specific threshold.

Pierce and Zilles found that InvToken found the most instances of plagiarism, at 73%, followed closely by InvIdents at 67%. Interestingly, their overlap was only 50%, meaning that all or almost all instances were detected by one of those two tools. That makes the combination of those two tools very effective in detecting plagiarism.

The biggest limiting factor of MOSS-like tools is that they only compare submissions against the contents of a database provided by the instructor (usually consisting of all current student submissions as well as historical submissions from prior years). This neglects two important sources of plagiarism. First, a student can still hire another student (either locally or on the internet) to complete their work. Second, they could obtain code from a source not included in the database. As such, it is important to remember (as stated on the MOSS website) that "Moss is not a system for completely automatically detecting plagiarism. Plagiarism is a statement that someone copied code deliberately without attribution, and while Moss automatically detects program similarity, it has no way of knowing *why* codes are similar" (Alex Aiken (n.d.)). Algae's measures have the same limitation – they are all between-submission comparisons.

Despite this limitation, detectors are effective at detecting many instances of possible plagiarism. For example, Chen et al. (2024) found that about 20% of students had plagiarism indicators present in 10% of their submissions prior to GenAI, with that rising to about 35% afterwards.

In light of MOSS-like tools' behavior, specifically checking for code similarity, assignments must be of sufficient complexity that wide variation in solutions is expected. For very simple coding exercises, it is likely that many students will independently generate the same solution, especially one that aligns with the way the material was taught in class.

However, there is one characteristic of GenAI that could make detection challenging for MOSS-like tools – the variation in results. Prior work found that MOSS was not effective at detecting unauthorized use of GenAI on early coding assignments (Biderman and Raff 2022). This is in contrast to Chen et al. detecting more plagiarism with their more varied techniques. While students often employ obfuscation techniques that MOSS can detect (moving code around and changing names), the authentic variation within code produced by GenAI tools makes this more difficult. To understand why, we must recall that LLMs are essentially nondeterministic (even when their temperature values are set to zero) and the models are extremely sensitive to differences in prompts. Further research is warranted to discover the nature of variation in GenAI coding results compared with the natural variation in student solutions.

A promising alternative approach from the realm of plagiarism detection that might be more effective at detecting unauthorized use of GenAI code is to shift the focus from the *final artifact* being submitted to the *code development process* through which students generated the solutions. In particular, when students use plagiarized code (whether from GenAI or traditional sources), they tend to copy large segments of completed code at a time rather than iteratively building up to a solution. By analyzing the intermediate steps before a student arrived at the final implementation, whether in the form of code commits (Reid and Wilson 2005) or even keystroke data (Hart, Mano, and Edwards 2023), it is possible to flag instances of large segments of polished code materializing for deeper scrutiny. However, this type of surveillance raises privacy concerns and has been shown to increase student stress (Hart et al. 2023).

Deep learning approaches specifically crafted to identify LLM-generated solutions have also shown promise. Hoq et al. (2024) explored the efficacy of deep learning models trained to detect ChatGPT-generated code for CS1 assignments and found them to be effective with an accuracy of above 90%. However, the authors note that the model tended to focus on programming patterns displaying knowledge beyond what a novice programmer might be familiar with and question whether the approach would be as effective in more advanced courses.

7.2 Learning Impacts from Misuse

The potential learning impacts from misuse of Gen AI tools cannot be underestimated. As with any field, courses build up knowledge and skills gradually through a carefully designed sequence of tasks. Any method by which a student completes tasks without gaining the associated knowledge and skill places them at a disadvantage in future courses, making them more reliant on plagiarism to succeed. This vicious cycle becomes more difficult to break the longer they stay in it, as the gap between their skills and the expected set of skills grows.

One could imagine a positive learning path for a student who, when the task was posed, was unable to generate the code accurately. They could generate the code and then inspect it to understand it, identifying what they were unable to generate. If seeing the code was not sufficient, they could then ask GenAI for a code explanation, and perhaps that would provide the extra information they needed. Is this a likely scenario?

We first look at the relationship between plagiarism and learning loss prior to GenAI. Detected learning loss due to plagiarism within computer science courses was small but statistically significant. Pierce and Zilles (2017) found only marginal, though statistically significant, learning loss (0.89 points on a 0–12 point scale). However, when breaking down the results by the number of assignments students plagiarized, they find a greater impact for students who plagiarized at least four assignments. Similarly, in a large-scale data analysis of student work, Chen et al. (2024) calculated that a student observed to plagiarize all four assignments would be expected to perform 47 points lower on the final exam prior to GenAI and 36 points lower afterwards (the difference between the 47 and 36 points was not statistically significant). Kazemitabaar et al.'s study (2023) also shows a clear trend that students with access to Codex (integrated within an IDE) submitted AI-generated code around half of the time without making any changes to it. It is likely that a student who merely generated the code and submitted it without inspecting it (say, to an automated testing system that provided a score) would learn nothing from the exercise.

However, evidence from recent studies suggests that the reality might be more complex. Prather et al. (2024) observed that while some students can effectively leverage GenAI tools like GitHub Copilot and ChatGPT to accelerate their learning and problem-solving processes, others struggle significantly, often leading to an "illusion of competence." Students who struggle may find themselves reliant on the AI's output, potentially compounding existing metacognitive difficulties and even introducing new ones. As a result, rather than facilitating learning, GenAI could inadvertently widen the gap between well-performing and poorly performing students.

Therefore, while there is no definitive answer on the exact effect of GenAI-based plagiarism on learning loss, there is evidence based on student behavior (not modifying what they receive), student attitudinal outcomes (an illusion of competence), and large-scale data analyses (exam performance) that indicates substantial learning loss when students utilize GenAI inappropriately.

7.3 Designing Courses to Avoid Misuse

Course design involves a plethora of elements – assignments, assessments, and overall course policies. In this subsection, we consider what researchers have proposed to encourage productive use of GenAI.

ChatGPT-Proofing Assignments

A common immediate reaction to the challenges posed by unauthorized use of GenAI is the idea of "ChatGPT-Proofing" assignments: by identifying tasks at which LLMs have been observed to perform poorly and incorporating these into assignments, educators hope to discourage unauthorized use of GenAI or at the very least ensure that students are unable to earn full credit solely by relying on code generated through GenAI. Unfortunately, the rapid improvement of LLMs in recent years, coupled with the diverse range of problems they can solve, makes it difficult to devise challenges that are consistently beyond the capabilities of these models.

Using CS-1 tasks as an example: Savelka, Agarwal, An et al. (2023) analyzed the performance of GPT-3, GPT-3.5, and GPT-4 using actual CS-1 course material and found that while prior generations of GPT were unable to earn passing grades, GPT-4 was able to consistently earn passing scores on assignments to such an extent that students who relied exclusively on GenAI for their solutions would have been able to score a passing grade. Therefore, while it might still be possible to redesign elements of a course to be "ChatGPT-proof," having to redesign a course every time there is an improvement in GenAI technology is not sustainable.

Alternative approaches recognize the futility of trying to "outsmart" GenAI systems. Instead, they propose changing the nature of the assignments themselves to create tasks where the use of GenAI would not be advantageous, or even possible. These changes could include emphasizing learning outcomes that can't be achieved by copying code. This could include focusing on outcomes such as understanding software development processes, conceptual knowledge, problem-solving skills, and other areas that require active student engagement.

As LLMs can produce correct code for almost any CS1-level problem if that problem is clearly specified, one novel approach to designing tasks that are less vulnerable to this issue is the concept of "probeable problems" as proposed by Pawagi et al. (2024). The motivation for this work stems from the challenge that beginner-level programming problems in competitive contexts often become trivial when participants use AI tools like GitHub Copilot or ChatGPT. The basic idea behind probeable problems is that certain details are deliberately omitted from the problem statement, making it difficult for an LLM to solve the task simply by analyzing the provided prompt. Instead, a mechanism is provided that allows students to probe or query the problem to uncover additional information about the desired behavior, using what the authors describe as "clarifying questions." This approach not only hinders the straightforward use of AI tools but also encourages students to engage more deeply with the problem, much like a developer would need to elicit specific requirements from a client in real-world scenarios. A trivial example might be to ask students to write a function (that takes an array or a list of integers as input, as well as two additional inputs, a and b) that: "Counts how many values are between 'a' and 'b' in the array". In this case, the problem does not specify whether to be counted a value must be strictly greater than a and strictly less than b (or indeed strictly greater than b and strictly less than a), or whether they can be equal to these boundary values. The student can find the answer to these questions by submitting clarifying questions in the way of test cases that are given to an oracle (a model solution to the problem) and for which the output can be observed.

In their paper, Pawagi and Kumar (2024) evaluated this approach by conducting a programming contest with undergraduate students. They found that popular AI tools were unable to generate correct solutions for the probeable problems due to the missing details, validating the effectiveness of this approach. However, while students were generally able to handle some of the omissions, they struggled with more complex cases, determining only around 20% of the missing details. This suggests that some further refinement of the problems or additional practice with this type of task could be useful. Another useful avenue for future work would involve exploring how to better support students in developing the skill of probing or querying to clarify ambiguous problem statements.

Adjusting Grade Distributions

Another approach is shifting the grade distribution to increase the focus on in-person tests/assessments where students cannot use GenAI: if students are aware that the bulk of their grade will be determined by assessments in which they will be unable to use tools such as ChatGPT, they may be less likely to use them to such an extent that they become dependent on them, even when they believe there is little risk of being caught. This approach has been proposed to combat plagiarism as early as 1982 (Hwang and Gibson 1982). If exams become more heavily weighted, there are two approaches.

The first is already followed by European universities – the bulk of the term is spent performing tasks that prepare a student for exams at the end of that term. Unfortunately, a model in which students are expected to perform a lot of work with little reward, all in preparation for a large reward at the end, does not follow behavioral theories related to motivation. Goal-setting theory claims that difficult, specific, context-appropriate, and immediate goals, rather than long-term goals, motivate learners to achieve more (Ling et al. 2005). In addition, it reduces the number of samples of student performance and can increase test anxiety (Zeidner 1998). Therefore, learning goals need to be cut up into small chunks, with points and badges for intermediate progress. In addition, effective feedback is timely, and waiting until the end of the term to provide substantive feedback would not allow students to adjust their behavior sufficiently.

The second model is frequent testing; however, this can be a burden on instructional staff. On top of the challenge related to writing additional assessment questions, there is the logistical challenge of booking spaces for administering the tests. Paper-and-pencil tests are the primary mechanism for preventing use of online resources, as they eliminate the possibility of students using Gen AI tools, but they are time-consuming to grade. There has been recent growing interest in the idea of dedicated computer-based testing facilities which can overcome the logistical challenges (Zilles 2023). Emeka et al. (2024) describe a comparison of three different methods for administering computer-based tests at scale: (1) a dedicated Computer-Based Testing Center (CBTC), (2) Bring Your Own Device (BYOD) exams proctored in person in the classroom, and (3) BYOD exams proctored online via Zoom. Through randomized crossover experiments, they found that the testing modality did not significantly impact students' exam performance or study behaviors. However, they noted that different modalities offer varied logistical benefits and potential challenges. For instance, CBTCs provide a controlled environment that standardizes the testing experience, while BYOD options, though more flexible, introduce security concerns and potential for increased cheating.

Adjusting Assessment Methodology

Dedicated computer-based testing facilities rely on large banks of questions from which a random subset is drawn for each individual student. Generating such large banks can be efficiently achieved using GenAI, which can create a wide variety of questions tailored to different levels of difficulty and topics. In a wonderful example of Universal Design, in which a solution to one problem leads to many unanticipated affordances, the capacity to generate individualized test questions enables much more than combating traditional cheating during an exam (i.e. students looking over each other's shoulders); it also enables a multitude of new testing modalities that have been shown to lead to positive student outcomes such as:

- **Asynchronous Testing**: By making it so that each test is unique to a student, there is no need to protect the integrity of the test by ensuring all students take the test at the same time; instead, instructors are able to define a time window during which time students can schedule their own test at the testing facility. This added flexibility enables students to take tests at whatever time works best for their schedules. More significantly, however, this makes it so that instructional time does not need to be sacrificed any time a test is administered.
- **Multiple Testing Attempts**: Given that each test is unique, students can be allowed to take the test multiple times, with each attempt generating a new batch of questions. This allows students to learn from their mistakes on the initial test and improve their understanding before reattempting and has been shown to greatly reduce the stress associated with tests.
- **Increased Testing Frequency**: Given that tests no longer eat away at instructional time, instructors can schedule multiple smaller tests throughout the semester rather than only a midterm and final as is conventional. By testing more often, students have more regular feedback about what they know and what they are struggling with, reducing the chance that they will have significant knowledge gaps by the end of the course. Furthermore, smaller, more frequent tests can be less anxiety-inducing than a handful of high-stakes assessments.
- **Mastery Learning**: Building on the idea of multiple testing attempts, instructors can set a grade threshold that students need to achieve to pass the course, with students given multiple opportunities to reach this mastery level. This approach encourages deeper understanding and learning, rather than rote memorization.

8 New and Emerging Pedagogical Approaches

Traditional pedagogical approaches, especially in introductory courses, have focused on helping students learn how to *write code*. This has commonly involved scaffolding tasks, like Parsons problems (Denny, Luxton-Reilly, and Simon 2008), code reading practice through code tracing (Venables, Tan, and

Lister 2009) or 'Explain in Plain English' problems (Murphy, McCauley, and Fitzgerald 2012), and frequent practice at writing code such as with 'many small problems' (Allen et al. 2019). Previous sections of this Element have focused on the impacts of GenAI when retaining the same learning goals. In this section, we consider whether the learning goals, or the priorities among different skills, might change with the emergence of GenAI. We ask the question, *Given the ease with which code can now be generated from natural language prompts, how does that change what we should teach?*

8.1 The Changing Industry Landscape

To answer this question, we first consider how GenAI is already changing, and will further change, software developers' jobs. A GitHub survey reported that 92% of developers in the United States are using GenAI tools, and 70% of them perceive benefits such as upskilling and increased productivity (Shani 2023).

How does coding change when one has a GenAI helper such as Copilot? There are two main phases when coding with Copilot. First, the developer needs to formulate a prompt so that Copilot can produce code that matches the desired functionality as closely as possible. Copilot can create a draft of the code, albeit potentially with bugs or otherwise not satisfying the desired requirements. Second, once the draft code has been produced, the developer's primary job is to assess and potentially modify the code. Thus, code reading, comprehension, and debugging skills are essential – more essential than writing code from a blank screen. So, not only do code modification skills become more important, skills applicable only to coding without a GenAI helper become less important.

We now explore two novel pedagogical approaches driven by these changing needs. We also highlight their impact on accessibility, given the capabilities of LLMs for translating prompts written in a range of different natural languages.

8.2 Writing and Explaining Code by Prompting

We argue that the two major pedagogical changes are to explicitly teach prompt engineering for code-generating GenAI tools and emphasizing reading (and understanding) code over writing it.

Training students on how to craft effective prompts for code-generating models is a new skill. One approach for developing this skill is described by Denny, Leinonen et al. (2024) who introduce the idea of "Prompt Problems," a novel exercise designed to train students in the art of prompt creation. Prompt Problems require students to analyze visual or descriptive representations of programming tasks, formulate natural language prompts (which are used by an LLM to generate code), and validate the generated code against automated test cases. In their work, these problems were deployed using the "Promptly" tool in two introductory programming courses (CS1 and CS2), with promising results:

- Student Performance: Most students successfully solved the problems within a few attempts. For example, in both courses, around 75% of students successfully solved the first problem they were shown despite the tasks being ungraded. The number of words used by students in successful prompts varied greatly, suggesting that this is a skill that requires practice.
- Skill Development: Students reported that the activity enhanced their computational thinking skills, exposed them to new programming constructs, and reinforced their ability to logically break down problems. Many appreciated how Prompt Problems helped them focus on the high-level logic of programming rather than low-level syntax.
- Student Perceptions: While generally positive, some students expressed concerns about over-reliance on AI tools, and appeared somewhat anxious about their futures as computing professionals after observing how capable the models were at generating code. This finding in particular helps to emphasize the need for instructors to teach students the importance of adapting to the changing skills that are needed.

Reading and debugging code are not new skills, but they gain importance in the era of generative AI. As discussed previously, there are four common problem types used in programming courses – tracing, EiPE, Parsons Problems, and coding (code writing). Currently, tracing, EiPE, and coding questions are commonly used for quizzes and exams, whereas Parsons Problems and coding are primarily used as homework exercises. In each case, writing code from scratch is often considered the end goal of the sequence. With the emergence of GenAI, the importance of tracing and debugging increases dramatically.

Explain in Plain English (EiPE) problems, traditionally used to develop code comprehension skills, have gained renewed relevance. In these tasks, students articulate the purpose of a given code segment in natural language. One of the biggest problems with deploying EiPE questions has been the need to manually grade student solutions (which are typically short fragments of plain text). Smith et al. (2024) proposed a system where student-generated explanations are used as prompts for LLMs to generate equivalent code, which is then tested against predefined test cases. This approach enables automated assessment and feedback while maintaining transparency. Key findings of an evaluation of this approach, involving nearly 900 students, include the following:

- Enhanced Feedback: Students benefit from viewing both the generated code and test results, which help them refine their explanations.
- Improved Engagement: Students valued the opportunity to align their natural language understanding with computational logic. For example, many noted that small changes in their wording led to significant differences in generated outputs, fostering a deeper understanding of the relationship between problem statements and code.
- Pedagogical Impact: The immediacy of feedback and the support for iterative development of solutions supports a shift from merely assessing code comprehension to actively teaching it, making these questions appropriate for formative learning.

A major advantage of these pedagogical approaches is their potential to make computing education more accessible to learners for whom English is not their native language. Given the natural language translation capabilities of LLMs, both Prompt Problems and EiPE tasks can support prompts written in multiple languages, allowing students to engage with programming concepts in their native language (D. H. Smith, Kumar, and Denny 2024). This feature significantly lowers the barrier to entry for nonnative English speakers, opening the doors to computer science and programming for a broader and more diverse range of learners.

9 CS1-LLM: A Case Study of LLM Integration in an Introductory Coding Course

We now present a case study of a newly designed course for introductory coding, as described by Vadaparty et al. (2024). This course reimagines what computer science education could look like when embracing GenAI tools, such as GitHub Copilot, fully and deliberately from the outset. The authors describe the rationale for this new approach by emphasizing two key reasons for redesigning introductory programming courses around LLMs. First, with the increasing capabilities of LLMs for generating code, traditional skills like writing code from scratch may no longer hold the same priority. Tools like Github Copilot are now widely adopted in industry,[5] and thus explicit instruction in using such tools will better prepare students for the workforce. Second, integrating LLMs allows students to engage more quickly in larger, open-ended projects that are personally relevant, thereby improving engagement. This is in contrast to more traditional CS1 approaches, where there is a considerable

---

[5] https://github.blog/news-insights/research/survey-reveals-ais-impact-on-the-developer-experience/

early focus on syntax and lower-level details that constrain students to working on small problems that are often less reflective of real-world software development.

The CS1-LLM approach allows students to focus more on core computational thinking skills such as problem decomposition, code analysis, and debugging, while also learning to interact with LLMs – a skill that is becoming essential in modern software development.

Design Principles

Vadaparty et al. (2024) describe several design principles underpinning the CS1-LLM approach. These include incorporating LLMs throughout the coursework, including on some final assessments. They note that there is not yet consensus in the community about the fundamental skills that should be learned with and without LLMs, and thus there remain some aspects of the course in which students are expected to write some code without the support of LLMs. However, given that reading and modifying code is an essential skill in industry, most assessments allowed students to start by generating code using Github Copilot. The course was also designed to support diverse learners by leveraging best practices from the computing education literature, such as the use of Peer Instruction, media computation, and pair programming, which are known to enhance engagement and retention. Another core principle was to foster creativity by providing students with opportunities to engage in open-ended projects that are personally relevant. Finally, the course was crafted to serve both students who would continue in computer science and those who might not take further computing courses, but who would benefit from being able to write programs to solve real problems in other domains. This resulted in a course that focused less on low-level syntax, and more on providing students the skills to leverage powerful libraries for automating mundane tasks such as processing large quantities of data.

Tool Support

An interesting aspect of the course, aligned with the first design principle, was the introduction of GitHub Copilot from the very beginning. Students were taught how to install and use Copilot within the Visual Studio Code IDE during the first week of the course. They began creating programs by typing English comments and allowing Copilot to generate the corresponding Python code. This approach is essentially the same as the "sketch model" of collaboration between humans and AI as proposed by Alves and Cipriano (2023), where the programmer provides the outline, and the AI fills in the gaps. The instructors used this as an opportunity to teach Python syntax and programming concepts, gradually building students' understanding of how to collaborate effectively with AI tools including for learning support. For example in lectures, students were shown how to use Copilot Chat, which is similar to ChatGPT but is integrated directly into VS Code and thus has access to the code being developed.

Learning Objectives and Resources

The learning goals of the course were designed to reflect the integration of LLMs. The revised goals focused on skills such as prompt engineering, code analysis, testing, debugging, and problem decomposition. Traditional objectives like writing code from scratch were de-emphasized, while new objectives like applying prompt engineering to influence AI-generated code were introduced (Denny, Kumar, and Giacaman 2023).

A novel component of the course was the introduction of a "function design cycle," which outlines a process for students to follow from crafting a prompt, generating code with Copilot, and then evaluating and debugging that code. The course also utilized the textbook by Porter and Zingaro (2023), titled *Learn AI-Assisted Python Programming with GitHub Copilot and ChatGPT*, which was written to accompany the course.

Vadaparty et al. (2024) present an evaluation of this approach with more than 500 students. The evaluation involved surveying students on their perceptions of the new course structure. While the majority of students responded positively, appreciating the creativity and scale of the projects, some challenges were noted. These included concerns about over-reliance on Copilot and some confusion from students about what they should be able to do with and without the support of an LLM.

Open-Ended Projects

The use of Copilot enabled more ambitious and interesting projects than students usually complete in their first introductory coding course. Students engaged in three open-ended projects across different domains:

- **Data Science** Students were tasked with finding a dataset on Kaggle,[6] identifying a question that could be answered with that data, and writing code to explore the answer.

---

[6] www.kaggle.com/

- **Image Manipulation** Students created a collage by manipulating images, demonstrating their understanding of Python's image processing capabilities.
- **Game Design** Students designed and implemented a text-based game or a game simulation, showcasing their creativity and programming skills.

These projects aligned with culturally relevant teaching pedagogy, allowing students to choose personally meaningful topics. Students generally reported finding the projects helpful for their learning, and feedback from students indicated that although the projects were sometimes challenging, they were highly memorable.

Assessment Methodology

In CS1-LLM, quizzes primarily excluded the use of Copilot, focusing on foundational skills like code tracing, explanation, and small coding tasks. In the final exam, Copilot was integrated into the third section for solving a large, open-ended problem, while the second section required students to complete four code-writing tasks of increasing difficulty without Copilot, emphasizing a balance between traditional coding skills and effective AI tool usage.

One of the most significant changes introduced in the CS1-LLM course was in the assessment methods for coding projects. Traditionally, coding assignments in introductory programming courses are graded using automated test cases. In this conventional approach, instructional staff invest time in setting up these test cases, but the actual grading process is largely automated and focuses on whether the student's code produces the correct output under a predefined set of conditions.

However, with the integration of tools like GitHub Copilot, which can generate code for projects at the CS1 level, this traditional approach to grading becomes less effective. If students are using Copilot to generate code, simply checking the correctness of outputs through automated tests no longer sufficiently assesses the students' understanding and skills. Recognizing this, the assessment methods were redesigned to focus more on the students' ability to explain and justify their work, rather than just the final product.

In the new assessment framework, students were required to submit not only their code but also a comprehensive diagram illustrating the decomposition of their program. This diagram served as a visual representation of their problem-solving process, showing how they broke down the problem into manageable functions and how those functions interacted within the overall structure of the program.

In addition to the diagram, students were also required to produce a five-minute video presentation of their project. This video had to include at least three minutes dedicated to explaining the details of one specific function within their code. This aspect of the assessment was crucial because it allowed students to demonstrate their understanding of the underlying logic and functionality of their code, rather than relying solely on the code's output.

The grading of each project was thus a more holistic process, taking into account not only the correctness of the code but also the student's ability to effectively communicate their thought process and the structure of their solution. Each project took approximately 10–15 minutes to grade, during which instructors carefully reviewed the code, evaluated the decomposition diagram, and assessed the clarity and depth of the student's explanation in the video. This approach emphasized the development of critical thinking and problem-solving skills in addition to technical proficiency.

Looking ahead, the authors suggest several areas for improvement in future iterations of the CS1-LLM course. These include providing clearer guidance to students on when and how to use Copilot, refining the balance between AI-assisted and independent coding tasks, and continuing to explore ways to better support diverse learners.

Alignment to Prior Research

The integration of GenAI in the assessments and pedagogy of the CS1-LLM course aligns closely with the principles and challenges outlined throughout this Element. First, the open-ended nature of the projects aligns with the guidance discussed in Section 7.3, particularly given the limitations of LLMs in handling problems that are not clearly specified in detail. The assessment approach, which includes students preparing video presentations of their unique projects, emphasizes critical skills such as communication and problem-solving over merely producing code that satisfies predefined requirements.

The design of the quizzes and exams in CS1-LLM reflects a balance between promoting traditional programming skills and allowing strategic use of GenAI. Quizzes excluded Copilot, focusing on foundational skills like code tracing, explanation, Parsons Problems, and small coding tasks. The final exam included four code-writing tasks where students worked without Copilot, as well as one larger question to be completed with Copilot. This frequent short quizzing and a structured, controlled exam addresses concerns about over-reliance on AI as discussed in Section 3.

Finally, the instructional emphasis on prompt engineering and debugging directly addresses the evolving skill sets identified in Section 8. By recognizing the growing importance of these skills in the presence of GenAI, CS1-LLM exemplifies a forward-looking approach to curriculum design, preparing students for both current industry needs and future developments.

10 Conclusions

In this Element, we have explored some of the many ways that large language models have and will continue to impact computer science education. We have seen that LLMs (and an emerging suite of LLM-powered tools) are capable of generating high-quality instructional materials and providing round-the-clock support to students. However, they also raise significant concerns, including potential misuse such as over-reliance and plagiarism.

Large language models show great promise for transforming how educators prepare and deliver their courses. For instance, LLMs can dynamically create culturally relevant assignments, efficiently modify problems to enable reuse, and produce personalized learning resources that align with diverse student needs and interests. These capabilities suggest a future where educational materials can be highly adaptive, relevant, and engaging, while reducing the preparation time for educators.

However, we have also discussed a number of challenges that require thoughtful consideration. Academic integrity is at the forefront, as LLMs make it easier for students to bypass learning processes either deliberately or as a result of poor metacognitive skills. For students in formal classes or learning on their own, chat-based agents like ChatGPT are promising in their ability to explain concepts at different levels of complexity, help students identify and diagnose errors in their work, and contextualize content to suit individual interests. The CS1-LLM case study demonstrated that it is possible to embrace LLMs in an introductory programming setting in a way that is well received by learners.

Large language models are clearly a transformative technology, but they are also just one more step in a long line of technological innovations that have affected computer science education – personal computers, the internet, large-scale automation, and now LLMs. Each technology has provided benefits by making information and instructional materials more accessible and easier to create, while at the same time providing new avenues for academic misconduct. Will LLMs eventually become capable of autonomously guiding students through complex coding tasks, providing detailed and personalized feedback on learning progression, and even detecting plagiarism with high accuracy? The potential for LLMs to fundamentally reshape learning environments is vast, but this requires a collective effort to explore and establish best practices.

As the CS1-LLM case study illustrates, fully embracing LLMs leads to a variety of changes in a course, especially from the student perspective. The creators of the CS1-LLM work note, however, that the changes were not as extensive as they originally anticipated (Vadaparty et al. 2024). With the right technological help, will universities and instructors put in the time and money to create courses that reimagine computer science instruction, from the learning goals to the assignments to the assessment techniques? Only time will tell.

References

Aiken, A. (n.d.). *A System for Detecting Software Similarity.* Accessed June 24, 2024, at https://theory.stanford.edu/~aiken/moss/

Alkafaween, U., Albluwi, I., & Denny, P. (2024). Automating autograding: Large language models as test suite generators for introductory programming. https://arxiv.org/abs/2411.09261

Allen, J. M., Vahid, F., Downey, K., Miller, K., & Edgcomb, A. D. (2019). Many small programs in CS1: Usage analysis from multiple universities. In *2019 ASEE Annual Conference & Exposition.* https://monolith.asee.org/public/conferences/140/papers/27535/view

Allowatt, A., & Edwards, S. H. (2005). IDE support for test-driven development and automated grading in both Java and C++. In *Proceedings of the 2005 OOPSLA workshop on Eclipse technology eXchange* (pp. 100–104). New York, NY: Association for Computing Machinery. DOI: https://doi.org/10.1145/1117696.1117717

Alves, P., & Cipriano, B. P. (2023). The centaur programmer – how Kasparov's advanced chess spans over to the software development of the future. https://arxiv.org/abs/2304.11172

ASHP. (2023, Dec.). Study finds ChatGPT provides inaccurate responses to drug questions. https://news.ashp.org/News/ashp-news/2023/12/05/study-finds-chatgpt-provides-inaccurate-responses-to-drug-questions

Balse, R., Kumar, V., Prasad, P., & Warriem, J. M. (2023). Evaluating the quality of LLM-generated explanations for logical errors in CS1 student programs. In *Proceedings of the 16th Annual ACM India Compute Conference* (pp. 49–54). New York, NY: Association for Computing Machinery. DOI: https://doi.org/10.1145/3627217.3627233

Barr, A. (2023, Sept.). The summer is over, schools are back, and the data is in: ChatGPT is mainly a tool for cheating on homework. *Business Insider.* www.businessinsider.com/school-is-back-chatgpt-mainly-tool-cheating-homework-2023-9.

Becker, B. A., Denny, P., Finnie-Ansley, J., Luxton-Reilly, A., Prather, J., & Santos, E. A. (2023). Programming is hard – or at least it used to be: Educational opportunities and challenges of AI code generation. In *Proceedings of the 54th ACM Technical Symposium on Computer Science Education v. 1* (pp. 500–506). New York, NY: Association for Computing Machinery. DOI: https://doi.org/10.1145/3545945.3569759

Bernstein, S., Denny, P., Leinonen, J. et al. (2024). "Like a nesting doll": Analyzing recursion analogies generated by CS students using Large Language Models. DOI: https://doi.org/10.48550/arXiv.2403.09409.

Biderman, S., & Raff, E. (2022, Oct.). Fooling MOSS detection with pretrained language models. In *Proceedings of the 31st ACM International Conference on Information & Knowledge Management* (pp. 2933–2943). New York, NY: Association for Computing Machinery. DOI: https://doi.org/10.1145/3511808.3557079

Chen, B., Lewis, C. M., West, M., & Zilles, C. (2024). Plagiarism in the age of generative AI: Cheating method change and learning loss in an Intro to CS course. In *Proceedings of the Eleventh ACM Conference on Learning@Scale* (pp. 75–85). New York, NY: Association for Computing Machinery. DOI: https://doi.org/10.1145/3657604.3662046

Chen, M., Tworek, J., Jun, H. et al. (2021). Evaluating large language models trained on code. https://arxiv.org/abs/2107.03374

Cipriano, B. P., & Alves, P. (2023). GPT-3 vs object oriented programming assignments: An experience report. In *Proceedings of the 2023 Conference on Innovation and Technology in Computer Science Education v. 1* (pp. 61–67). New York, NY: Association for Computing Machinery. DOI: https://doi.org/10.1145/3587102.3588814

Corder, M. (2024, Aug.). Clearview AI fined $33.7 million by Dutch data protection watchdog over "illegal database" of faces. Associated Press. https://apnews.com/article/clearview-ai-facial-recognition-privacy-fine-netherlands-a1ac33c15d561d37a923b6c382f48ab4

Coyle, J. (2023, Sept.). In Hollywood writers' battle against AI, humans win (for now). *Associated Press*. https://apnews.com/article/hollywood-ai-strike-wga-artificial-intelligence-39ab72582c3a15f77510c9c30a45ffc8.

Crow, T., Luxton-Reilly, A., & Wuensche, B. (2018). Intelligent tutoring systems for programming education: A systematic review. In *Proceedings of the 20th Australasian Computing Education Conference* (pp. 53–62). New York, NY: Association for Computing Machinery. DOI: https://doi.org/10.1145/3160489.3160492

Davis, K., White, S. V., Dinah, B.- C., & Scott, A. (2021). *Culturally responsive-sustaining computer science education: A framework*. Kapor Center. www.kaporcenter.org/equitablecs

Del Carpio Gutierrez, A., Denny, P., & Luxton-Reilly, A. (2024). Evaluating automatically generated contextualised programming exercises. In *Proceedings of the 55th ACM Technical Symposium on Computer Science Education v. 1* (pp. 289–295). New York, NY: Association for Computing Machinery. DOI: https://doi.org/10.1145/3626252.3630863

Denny, P., Kumar, V., & Giacaman, N. (2023). Conversing with Copilot: Exploring prompt engineering for solving CS1 problems using natural language. In *Proceedings of the 54th ACM Technical Symposium on Computer Science Education v. 1* (pp. 1136–1142). New York, NY: Association for Computing Machinery. DOI: http://doi.org/10.1145/3545945.3569823

Denny, P., Leinonen, J., Prather, J. et al. (2024). Prompt problems: A new programming exercise for the generative AI era. In *Proceedings of the 55th ACM Technical Symposium on Computer Science Education v. 1* (pp. 296–302). New York, NY: Association for Computing Machinery. DOI: https://doi.org/10.1145/3626252.3630909

Denny, P., Luxton-Reilly, A., & Simon, B. (2008). Evaluating a new exam question: Parsons problems. In *Proceedings of the Fourth International Workshop on Computing Education Research* (pp. 113–124). New York, NY: Association for Computing Machinery. DOI: https://doi.org/10.1145/1404520.1404532

Denny, P., MacNeil, S., Savelka, J., Porter, L., & Luxton-Reilly, A. (2024). Desirable characteristics for AI teaching assistants in programming education. In *Proceedings of the 2024 Conference on Innovation and Technology in Computer Science Education v. 1* (pp. 408–414). New York, NY: Association for Computing Machinery. DOI: https://doi.org/10.1145/3649217.3653574

Denny, P., Prather, J., Becker, B. A. et al. (2019). A closer look at metacognitive scaffolding: Solving test cases before programming. In *Proceedings of the 19th Koli Calling International Conference on Computing Education Research.* New York, NY: Association for Computing Machinery. DOI: https://doi.org/10.1145/3364510.3366170

Denny, P., Prather, J., Becker, B. A. et al. (2024, Jan.). Computing education in the era of generative AI. *Communications of the ACM, 67*(2), 56–67. DOI: https://doi.org/10.1145/3624720

Denny, P., Smith, D. H., Fowler, M. et al. (2024). Explaining code with a purpose: An integrated approach for developing code comprehension and prompting skills. In *Proceedings of the 2024 Conference on Innovation and Technology in Computer Science Education v. 1* (pp. 283–289). New York, NY: Association for Computing Machinery. DOI: https://doi.org/10.1145/3649217.3653587.

DeVon, C. (2023, Nov.). *On ChatGPT's one-year anniversary, it has more than 1.7 billion users – here's what it may do next.* CNBC. www.cnbc.com/2023/11/30/chatgpts-one-year-anniversary-how-the-viral-ai-chatbot-has-changed.html

Ding, Z., Srinivasan, A., Macneil, S., & Chan, J. (2023). Fluid transformers and creative analogies: Exploring large language models' capacity for augmenting cross-domain analogical creativity. In *Proceedings of the 15th Conference on Creativity and Cognition* (pp. 489–505). New York, NY: Association for Computing Machinery. DOI: https://doi.org/10.1145/3591196.3593516

Duffy, H., & Weil, S. E. (2023, Feb.). *ChatGPT, Cheating, and the Future of Education.* The Harvard Crimson. www.thecrimson.com/article/2023/2/23/chatgpt-scrut/.

Edwards, B. (2023a, Jan.). *Artists File Class-Action Lawsuit against AI Image Generator Companies.* Ars Technica. https://arstechnica.com/information-technology/2023/01/artists-file-class-action-lawsuit-against-ai-image-generator-companies/.

Edwards, B. (2023b, Nov.). *ChatGPT Is One Year Old. Here's How It Changed the Tech World.* Ars Technica. https://arstechnica.com/information-techno logy/2023/11/chatgpt-was-the-spark-that-lit-the-fire-under-generative-ai-one-year-ago-today/.

Emeka, C., West, M., Zilles, C., & Silva, M. (2024). A comparison of proctoring regimens for computer-based computer science exams. In *Proceedings of the 2024 on Innovation and Technology in Computer Science Education v. 1* (pp. 185–191). New York, NY, USA: Association for Computing Machinery. DOI: https://doi.org/10.1145/3649217.3653536

Ericson, B. J., Denny, P., Prather, J. et al. (2022). Parsons problems and beyond: Systematic literature review and empirical study designs. In *Proceedings of the 2022 Working Group Reports on Innovation and Technology in Computer Science Education* (pp. 191–234). New York, NY: Association for Computing Machinery. DOI: https://doi.org/10.1145/3571785.3574127

Feng, D., Shaw, E., Kim, J., & Hovy, E. (2006). An intelligent discussion-bot for answering student queries in threaded discussions. In *Proceedings of the 11th International Conference on Intelligent User Interfaces* (pp. 171–177). New York, NY: Association for Computing Machinery. DOI: https://doi.org/10.1145/1111449.1111488

Finnie-Ansley, J., Denny, P., Becker, B. A., Luxton-Reilly, A., & Prather, J. (2022). The robots are coming: Exploring the implications of openai codex on introductory programming. In *Proceedings of the 24th Australasian Computing Education Conference* (pp. 10–19). New York, NY: Association for Computing Machinery. DOI: https://doi.org/10.1145/3511861.3511863

Finnie-Ansley, J., Denny, P., Luxton-Reilly, A. et al. (2023). My AI wants to know if this will be on the exam: Testing OpenAI's Codex on CS2 programming exercises. In *Proceedings of the 25th Australasian Computing Education Conference* (pp. 97–104). New York, NY: Association for Computing Machinery. DOI: https://doi.org/10.1145/3576123.3576134

Fisler, K. (2014). The recurring rainfall problem. In *Proceedings of the Tenth Annual Conference on International Computing Education Research* (pp. 35–42). New York, NY: Association for Computing Machinery. DOI: https://doi.org/10.1145/2632320.2632346

Fowler, M., Smith, D. H., & Zilles, C. (2024). Quickly producing "isomorphic" exercises: Quantifying the impact of programming question permutations. In *Proceedings of the 2024 on Innovation and Technology in Computer Science Education v. 1* (pp. 178–184). New York, NY: Association for Computing Machinery. DOI: https://doi.org/10.1145/3649217.3653617

Franklin, D., Conrad, P., Boe, B. et al. (2013). Assessment of computer science learning in a scratch-based outreach program. In *Proceeding of the 44th ACM Technical Symposium on Computer Science Education* (pp. 371–376). New York, NY: Association for Computing Machinery. DOI: https://doi.org/10.1145/2445196.2445304

Franklin, D., Weintrop, D., Palmer, J. et al. (2020). Scratch encore: The design and pilot of a culturally-relevant intermediate scratch curriculum. In *Proceedings of the 51st ACM Technical Symposium on Computer Science Education* (pp. 794–800).

Gay, G. (2018). *Culturally Responsive Teaching: Theory, Research, and Practice.* Teachers College Press.

Gonzalez-Maldonado, D., Liu, J., & Franklin, D. (2025). Evaluating GPT for use in K–12 block based CS instruction using a transpiler and prompt engineering. In *Proceedings of the 56th ACM Technical Symposium on Computer Science Education v. 1.*

Hart, K., Mano, C., & Edwards, J. (2023, March). Plagiarism deterrence in CS1 through keystroke data. In *Proceedings of the 54th ACM Technical Symposium on Computer Science Education V. 1* (pp. 493–499). New York, NY: Association for Computing Machinery. DOI: https://doi.org/10.1145/3545945.3569805

Hattie, J., & Timperley, H. (2007). The power of feedback. *Review of Educational Research, 77*(1), 81–112. DOI: https://doi.org/10.3102/003465430298487

Hicke, Y., Agarwal, A., Ma, Q., & Denny, P. (2023). *Ai-ta: Towards an intelligent question-answer teaching assistant using open-source LLMs.* Available at https://arxiv.org/abs/2311.02775

Hoq, M., Shi, Y., Leinonen, J. et al. (2024, March). Detecting ChatGPT-generated code submissions in a CS1 course using machine learning models. In *Proceedings of the 55th ACM Technical Symposium on Computer Science Education V. 1* (pp. 526–532). New York, NY: Association for Computing Machinery. DOI: https://doi.org/10.1145/3626252.3630826

Hou, I., Man, O., Mettille, S. et al. (2024). More robots are coming: Large multimodal models (ChatGPT) can solve visually diverse images of Parsons problems. In *Proceedings of the 26th Australasian Computing Education Conference* (p. 29–38). New York, NY: Association for Computing Machinery. DOI: https://doi.org/10.1145/3636243.3636247

Hwang, C. J., & Gibson, D. E. (1982, Feb.). Using an effective grading method for preventing plagiarism of programming assignments. *SIGCSE Bulletin*, *14*(1), 50–59.

Johnson, K. (2023, Feb.). *Face recognition software led to his arrest. it was dead wrong; Alonzo Sawyer's misidentification by algorithm made him a suspect for a crime police now say was committed by someone else – feeding debate over regulation.* Wired. https://www.wired.com/story/face-recognition-software-led-to-his-arrest-it-was-dead-wrong/

Jury, B., Lorusso, A., Leinonen, J., Denny, P., & Luxton-Reilly, A. (2024). Evaluating LLM-generated worked examples in an introductory programming course. In *Proceedings of the 26th Australasian Computing Education Conference* (p. 77–86). New York, NY: Association for Computing Machinery. DOI: https://doi.org/10.1145/3636243.3636252

Katersky, A. (2023, Nov.). *Famous authors' lawsuit against ChatGPT developer gets underway.* ABC News. https://abcnews.go.com/US/famous-authors-lawsuit-chatgpt-maker-openai-begins-initial/story?id=105239215#:~:text=A20group20of20well2Dknown,train20the20popular20chatbot20ChatGPT. ABCNews.

Kazemitabaar, M., Chow, J., Ma, C. K. T. et al. (2023). Studying the effect of AI code generators on supporting novice learners in introductory programming. In *Proceedings of the 2023 CHI Conference on Human Factors in Computing Systems.* New York, NY: Association for Computing Machinery. DOI: https://doi.org/10.1145/3544548.3580919

Kotek, H., Dockum, R., & Sun, D. (2023). Gender bias and stereotypes in large language models. In *Proceedings of the ACM Collective Intelligence Conference* (pp. 12–24).

Ladson-Billings, G. (1995). Toward a theory of culturally relevant pedagogy. *American Educational Research Journal*, *32*(3), 465–491.

Lau, S., & Guo, P. (2023). From "ban it till we understand it" to "resistance is futile": How university programming instructors plan to adapt as more students use AI code generation and explanation tools such as ChatGPT and Github Copilot. In *Proceedings of the 2023 ACM Conference on International Computing Education Research – Volume 1* (pp. 106–121). New York, NY: Association for Computing Machinery. DOI: https://doi.org/10.1145/3568813.3600138

Leinonen, J., Denny, P., MacNeil, S. et al. (2023). Comparing code explanations created by students and large language models. In *Proceedings of the 2023 Conference on Innovation and Technology in Computer Science Education v. 1* (pp. 124–130). New York, NY: Association for Computing Machinery. DOI: https://doi.org/10.1145/3587102.3588785

Leinonen, J., Denny, P., & Whalley, J. (2021). Exploring the effects of contextualized problem descriptions on problem solving. In *Proceedings of the 23rd Australasian Computing Education Conference* (pp. 30–39). New York, NY: Association for Computing Machinery. DOI: https://doi.org/10.1145/3441636.3442302

Leinonen, J., Hellas, A., Sarsa, S. et al. (2023, March). Using large language models to enhance programming error messages. In *Proceedings of the 54th ACM Technical Symposium on Computer Science Education V. 1* (pp. 563–569). New York, NY: Association for Computing Machinery. DOI: https://doi.org/10.1145/3545945.3569770

Liang, P. P., Wu, C., Morency, L.- P., & Salakhutdinov, R. (2021). Towards understanding and mitigating social biases in language models. In *International Conference on Machine Learning* (pp. 6565–6576).

Liffiton, M., Sheese, B. E., Savelka, J., & Denny, P. (2024). Codehelp: Using large language models with guardrails for scalable support in programming classes. In *Proceedings of the 23rd Koli Calling International Conference on Computing Education Research.* New York, NY: Association for Computing Machinery. DOI: https://doi.org/10.1145/3631802.3631830

Ling, K., Beenen, G., Ludford, P. et al. (2005). Using social psychology to motivate contributions to online communities. In *Proceedings of the 2004 ACM Conference on Computer Supported Cooperative Work* (pp. 212–221).

Lister, R., Simon, B., Thompson, E., Whalley, J. L., & Prasad, C. (2006). Not seeing the forest for the trees: Novice programmers and the solo taxonomy. In *Proceedings of the 11th Annual SIGCSE Conference on Innovation and Technology in Computer Science Education* (pp. 118–122). New York, NY: Association for Computing Machinery. DOI: https://doi.org/10.1145/1140124.1140157

Liu, M., & M'Hiri, F. (2024, March). Beyond Traditional Teaching: Large Language Models as Simulated Teaching Assistants in Computer Science. In *Proceedings of the 55th ACM Technical Symposium on Computer Science Education V. 1* (pp. 743–749). New York, NY: Association for Computing Machinery. DOI: https://doi.org/10.1145/3626252.3630789

MacNeil, S., Tran, A., Hellas, A. et al. (2023). Experiences from using code explanations generated by large language models in a web software development e-book. In *Proceedings of the 54th ACM Technical Symposium on Computer Science Education v. 1* (pp. 931–937). New York, NY: Association for Computing Machinery. DOI: https://doi.org/10.1145/3545945.3569785

Malone, T. W. (1981). Toward a theory of intrinsically motivating instruction. *Cognitive Science*, *5*(4), 333–369.

Margulieux, L. E., & Catrambone, R. (2016). Improving problem solving with subgoal labels in expository text and worked examples. *Learning and Instruction*, *42*, 58–71. Available at https://www.sciencedirect.com/science/article/pii/S095947521530044X DOI: https://doi.org/10.1016/j.learninstruc.2015.12.002

Margulieux, L. E., Catrambone, R., & Guzdial, M. (2016). Employing subgoals in computer programming education. *Computer Science Education*, *26*(1), 44–67. DOI: https://doi.org/10.1080/08993408.2016.1144429

Margulieux, L. E., Morrison, B. B., & Decker, A. (2020). Reducing withdrawal and failure rates in introductory programming with subgoal labeled worked examples. *International Journal on STEM Education*, *7*(19). Available at https://stemeducationjournal.springeropen.com/articles/10.1186/s40594-020-00222-7#citeas DOI: https://doi.org/10.1186/s40594-020-00222-7

Maslow, A. H. (1958). A dynamic theory of human motivation. doi: https://doi.org/10.1037/11305-004

Maslow, A. H. (1962). Lessons from the peak-experiences. *Journal of Humanistic Psychology*, *2*(1), 9–18.

McCabe, D., Trevino, L., & Butterfield, K. (2001). Cheating in academic institutions: A decade of research. *Ethics & Behavior*, *11*(3), 219.

Muldner, K., Jennings, J., & Chiarelli, V. (2022, Dec.). A review of worked examples in programming activities. *ACM Transactions on Computing Education*, *23*(1). DOI: https://doi.org/10.1145/3560266

Murphy, L., McCauley, R., & Fitzgerald, S. (2012). "Explain in plain English" questions: Implications for teaching. In *Proceedings of the 43rd ACM Technical Symposium on Computer Science Education* (pp. 385–390). New York, NY: Association for Computing Machinery. DOI: https://doi.org/10.1145/2157136.2157249

Nadeem, M., Bethke, A., & Reddy, S. (2020). Stereoset: Measuring stereotypical bias in pretrained language models. *arXiv:2004.09456*.

Neumeister, L. (2023, June). *Lawyers submitted bogus case law created by ChatGPT. A judge fined them $5,000*. Associated Press. https://apnews.com/article/artificial-intelligence-chatgpt-fake-case-lawyers-d6ae9fa79d0542db9e1455397aef381c.

Nguyen, H., & Allan, V. (2024, March). Using GPT-4 to provide tiered, formative code feedback. In *Proceedings of the 55th ACM Technical Symposium on Computer Science Education V. 1* (pp. 958–964). New York, NY: Association for Computing Machinery. DOI: https://doi.org/10.1145/3626252.3630960

Nietzel, M. T. (2023, March). *More than half of college students believe using ChatGPT to complete assignments is cheating.* Forbes. https://www.forbes.com/sites/michaeltnietzel/2023/03/20/more-than-half-of-college-students-believe-using-chatgpt-to-complete-assignments-is-cheating/

Notice to research community: Use of generative artificial intelligence technology in the nsf merit review process. (2023, Dec.). National Science Foundation. https://new.nsf.gov/news/notice-to-the-research-community-on-ai.

Opitz, B., Ferdinand, N., & Mecklinger, A. (2011). Timing matters: The impact of immediate and delayed feedback on artificial language learning. *Frontiers in Human Neuroscience, 5*(8). DOI: https://doi.org/10.3389/fnhum.2011.00008

Park, A., Kietzmann, J., Killoran, J. et al. (2023). Nothing is harder to resist than the temptation of AI. *IT Professional, 25*(6), 13-20. DOI: https://doi.org/10.1109/MITP.2023.3340529

Pawagi, M., & Kumar, V. (2024). Probeable problems for beginner-level programming-with-AI contests. In *Proceedings of the 2024 ACM Conference on International Computing Education Research – Volume 1* (pp. 166–176). New York, NY: Association for Computing Machinery. DOI: https://doi.org/10.1145/3632620.3671108

Petersen, A., Craig, M., & Zingaro, D. (2011). Reviewing CS1 exam question content. In *Proceedings of the 42nd ACM Technical Symposium on Computer Science Education* (pp. 631–636). New York, NY: Association for Computing Machinery. DOI: https://doi.org/10.1145/1953163.1953340

Pierce, J., & Zilles, C. (2017). Investigating student plagiarism patterns and correlations to grades. In *Proceedings of the 2017 ACM SIGCSE Technical Symposium on Computer Science Education* (pp. 471–476). New York, NY: Association for Computing Machinery. DOI: https://doi.org/10.1145/3017680.3017797

Porter, L., & Zingaro, D. (2023). *Learn AI-assisted Python programming with Github Copilot and ChatGPT.* Shelter Island, NY: Manning. Available at www.manning.com/books/learn-ai-assisted-python-programming

Powers, S. (2023, Feb.). *Vanderbilt university staff apologizes after ChatGPT was used to write email about MSU shooting.* CBS News. www.cbsnews.com/detroit/news/vanderbilt-university-staff-apologizes-after-chatgpt-was-used-to-write-email-about-msu-shooting/.

Pozdniakov, S., Brazil, J., Abdi, S. et al. (2024). Large language models meet user interfaces: The case of provisioning feedback. DOI: https://arxiv.org/abs/2404.11072

Prather, J., Denny, P., Leinonen, J. et al. (2023). The robots are here: Navigating the generative AI revolution in computing education. In *Proceedings of the 2023 Working Group Reports on Innovation and Technology in Computer Science Education* (pp. 108–159). New York, NY: Association for Computing Machinery. DOI: https://doi.org/10.1145/3623762.3633499

Prather, J., Reeves, B. N., Denny, P. et al. (2023, Nov.). "It's weird that it knows what I want": Usability and interactions with Copilot for novice programmers. *ACM Transactions on Computer–Human Interaction, 31*(1). DOI: https://doi.org/10.1145/3617367

Prather, J., Reeves, B. N., Leinonen, J. et al. (2024). The widening gap: The benefits and harms of generative AI for novice programmers. In *Proceedings of the 2024 ACM Conference on International Computing Education Research – Volume 1* (p. 469–486). New York, NY Association for Computing Machinery. DOI: https://doi.org/10.1145/3632620.3671116

Raj, A. G. S., Gu, P., Zhang, E. et al. (2020). Live-coding vs static code examples: Which is better with respect to student learning and cognitive load? In *Proceedings of the Twenty-Second Australasian Computing Education Conference* (pp. 152–159). New York, NY: Association for Computing Machinery. DOI: https://doi.org/10.1145/3373165.3373182

Reeves, B., Sarsa, S., Prather, J. et al. (2023). Evaluating the performance of code generation models for solving Parsons problems with small prompt variations. In *Proceedings of the 2023 Conference on Innovation and Technology in Computer Science Education v. 1* (pp. 299–305). New York, NY: Association for Computing Machinery. DOI: https://doi.org/10.1145/3587102.3588805

Reeves, B. N., Prather, J., Denny, P. et al. (2024). Prompts first, finally. DOI: https://arxiv.org/abs/2407.09231

Reid, K. L., & Wilson, G. V. (2005, Feb.). Learning by doing: Introducing version control as a way to manage student assignments. *SIGCSE Bulletin, 37*(1), 272–276. DOI: https://doi.org/10.1145/1047124.1047441

Rubin, M. J. (2013). The effectiveness of live-coding to teach introductory programming. In *Proceeding of the 44th ACM Technical Symposium on Computer Science Education* (pp. 651–656). New York, NY: Association for Computing Machinery. DOI: https://doi.org/10.1145/2445196.2445388

Sanders, K., & McCartney, R. (2016). Threshold concepts in computing: Past, present, and future. In *Proceedings of the 16th Koli Calling International Conference on Computing Education Research* (pp. 91–100). New

York, NY: Association for Computing Machinery. DOI: https://doi.org/10 .1145/2999541.2999546

Sanford, A. (2024, Feb.). Innocence Project. Available at https://innocence project.org/artificial-intelligence-is-putting-innocent-people-at-risk-of-being-incarcerated/

Sarsa, S., Denny, P., Hellas, A., & Leinonen, J. (2022). Automatic generation of programming exercises and code explanations using large language models. In *Proceedings of the 2022 ACM Conference on International Computing Education Research – Volume 1* (pp. 27–43). New York, NY: Association for Computing Machinery. DOI: https://doi.org/10.1145/3501385.3543957

Savelka, J., Agarwal, A., An, M., Bogart, C., & Sakr, M. (2023). Thrilled by your progress! Large language models (GPT-4) no longer struggle to pass assessments in higher education programming courses. In *Proceedings of the 2023 ACM Conference on International Computing Education Research – Volume 1* (pp. 78–92). New York, NY: Association for Computing Machinery. DOI: https://doi.org/10.1145/3568813.3600142

Savelka, J., Agarwal, A., Bogart, C., & Sakr, M. (2023). *From GPT-3 to GPT-4: On the evolving efficacy of LLMs to answer multiple-choice questions for programming classes in higher education.* arXiv:2311.09518 **[cs.CY]**

Shani, I. (2023). *Survey reveals AI's impact on the developer experience – the github blog.* Available at https://github.blog/2023-06-13-survey-reveals-ais-impact-onthe-developer-experience

Sheard, J., Denny, P., Hellas, A. et al. (2024). Instructor perceptions of AI code generation tools – a multi-institutional interview study. In *Proceedings of the 55th ACM Technical Symposium on Computer Science Education v. 1* (pp. 1223–1229). New York, NY: Association for Computing Machinery. DOI: https://doi.org/10.1145/3626252.3630880

Sheese, B., Liffiton, M., Savelka, J., & Denny, P. (2024). Patterns of student help-seeking when using a large language model-powered programming assistant. In *Proceedings of the 26th Australasian Computing Education Conference* (pp. 49–57). New York, NY: Association for Computing Machinery. DOI: https://doi.org/10.1145/3636243.3636249

Smith, A. J., Boyer, K. E., Forbes, J., Heckman, S., & Mayer-Patel, K. (2017). My digital hand: A tool for scaling up one-to-one peer teaching in support of computer science learning. In *Proceedings of the 2017 ACM SIGCSE Technical Symposium on CS Education* (pp. 549–554). NY: ACM. DOI: https://doi.org/10.1145/3017680.3017800

Smith, D. H., Denny, P., & Fowler, M. (2024). Prompting for comprehension: Exploring the intersection of explain in plain English questions and prompt writing. In *Proceedings of the Eleventh ACM Conference on Learning @*

Scale (pp. 39–50). New York, NY: Association for Computing Machinery. DOI: https://doi.org/10.1145/3657604.3662039

Smith, D. H., Kumar, V., & Denny, P. (2024). *Explain in plain language questions with Indic languages: Drawbacks, affordances, and opportunities.* https://arxiv.org/abs/2409.20297

Smith, D. H., & Zilles, C. (2023). *Code generation based grading: Evaluating an auto-grading mechanism for "explain-in-plain-English" questions.* https://arxiv.org/abs/2311.14903 (2023): n. pag.

Smith, M., Chen, Y., Berndtson, R., Burson, K. M., & Griffin, W. (2017). "Office hours are kind of weird": Reclaiming a resource to foster student–faculty interaction. *InSight: A Journal of Scholarly Teaching, 12*, 14–29.

Spector, C. (2023, Oct.). *What do AI chatbots really mean for students and cheating?* Stanford Graduate School of Education. Stanford Graduate School of Education. https://ed.stanford.edu/news/what-do-ai-chatbots-really-mean-students-and-cheating.

Stanly, M. (2023, Feb.). *A Colombian judge admits he used ChatGPT for the court ruling, which triggered public.* India AI. https://indiaai.gov.in/article/a-colombian-judge-admits-he-used-chatgpt-for-the-court-ruling-which-triggered-public.

Tao, Y., Viberg, O., Baker, R. S., & Kizilcec, R. F. (2024). Cultural bias and cultural alignment of large language models. *PNAS Nexus, 3*(9), pgae 346.

Taylor, A., Vassar, A., Renzella, J., & Pearce, H. (2024, March). dcc –help: Transforming the role of the compiler by generating context-aware error explanations with large language models. In *Proceedings of the 55th ACM Technical Symposium on Computer Science Education V. 1* (pp. 1314–1320). New York, NY: Association for Computing Machinery. DOI: https://doi.org/10.1145/3626252.3630822

Thorbecke, C. (2023, Nov.). *A year after ChatGPT's release, the AI revolution is just beginning.* CNN. https://www.cnn.com/2023/11/30/tech/chatgpt-openai-revolution-one-year/index.html.

Tran, M. (2023). Prompt engineering for large language models to support K–8 computer science teachers in creating culturally responsive projects. In *Proceedings of the 2023 ACM Conference on International Computing Education Research-Volume 2* (pp. 110–112).

Tran, M., Gonzalez-Maldonado, D., Zhou, E., & Franklin, D. (2025). Can GPT help? Supporting teachers to brainstorm customized instructional scratch projects. In *Proceedings of the 56th ACM Technical Symposium on Computer Science Education v. 1.*

Tran, M., Killen, H., Palmer, J., Weintrop, D., & Franklin, D. (2024). Harmonizing scratch encore: Scaffolding K–8 teachers in customizing culturally responsive computing materials. In *Proceedings of the 55th ACM Technical Symposium on Computer Science Education v. 1* (pp. 1335–1341).

Vadaparty, A., Zingaro, D., Smith IV, D. H. et al. (2024). CS1-LLM: Integrating LLMs into CS1 instruction. In *Proceedings of the 2024 on Innovation and Technology in Computer Science Education v. 1* (pp. 297–303). New York, NY: Association for Computing Machinery. DOI: https://doi.org/10.1145/3649217.3653584

Vellukunnel, M., Buffum, P., Boyer, K. E. et al. (2017). Deconstructing the discussion forum: Student questions and computer science learning. In *Proceedings of the 2017 ACM SIGCSE Technical Symposium on Computer Science Education* (pp. 603–608). New York, NY: Association for Computing Machinery. DOI: https://doi.org/10.1145/3017680.3017745

Venables, A., Tan, G., & Lister, R. (2009). A closer look at tracing, explaining and code writing skills in the novice programmer. In *Proceedings of the Fifth International Workshop on Computing Education Research Workshop* (pp. 117–128). New York, NY: Association for Computing Machinery. DOI: https://doi.org/10.1145/1584322.1584336

Verma, P. (2023, Oct). *ChatGPT provided better customer service than his staff. He fired them.* The Washington Post. www.washingtonpost.com/technology/2023/10/03/ai-customer-service-jobs/.

Vicci, G. (2023, Feb.). *ChatGPT making it easier for students to cheat in school.* CBS News. www.cbsnews.com/detroit/news/chatgpt-making-it-easier-for-students-to-cheat-in-school/.

Yang, S., Zhao, H., Xu, Y., Brennan, K., & Schneider, B. (2024, Aug.). Debugging with an AI tutor: Investigating novice help-seeking behaviors and perceived learning. In *Proceedings of the 2024 ACM Conference on International Computing Education Research* (Vol. 1, pp. 84–94). New York, NY: Association for Computing Machinery. DOI: https://doi.org/10.1145/3632620.3671092

Zamprogno, L., Holmes, R., & Baniassad, E. (2020, Nov.). Nudging student learning strategies using formative feedback in automatically graded assessments. In *Proceedings of the 2020 ACM SIGPLAN Symposium on SPLASH-E* (pp. 1–11). New York, NY: Association for Computing Machinery. DOI: https://doi.org/org/10.1145/3426431.3428654

Zeidner, M. (1998). *Test Anxiety: State of the Art*. Plenum Press.

Zhang, P., Jaipersaud, B., Ba, J. et al. (2023). Classifying course discussion board questions using LLMs. In *Proceedings of the 2023 Conference on Innovation and Technology in Computer Science Education v. 2* (p. 658).

New York, NY: Association for Computing Machinery. DOI: https://doi.org/10.1145/3587103.3594202

Zilles, C. (2023). Computer-based testing facilities as a means for enabling better assessment pedagogy. In *Proceedings of the 54th ACM Technical Symposium on Computer Science Education v. 2* (p. 1258). New York, NY: Association for Computing Machinery. DOI: https://doi.org/10.1145/3545947.3573226

Acknowledgments

We would like to thank all of the researchers for performing the work that informed this Element and the participants for being willing to use GenAI for experimental purposes. Some work was funded by the National Science Foundation, #DRL-2201313.

For EU product safety concerns, contact us at Calle de José Abascal, 56–1°,
28003 Madrid, Spain or eugpsr@cambridge.org.